Italian Frescoes

Italian Frescoes

Ernest Kurpershoek

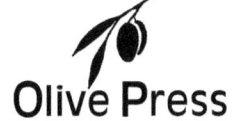
Olive Press

ISBN 9789077787427

© Ernest Kurpershoek 2014

Cover Design: Alfred Scheepers, using a fresco by Il Sodoma – Saint Benedict sends away the harlots. detail, Abbazia Monte Oliveto Maggiore. 1505-1508.

Translated from the Dutch by Karen Garmester and Alfred Scheepers

All rights reserved. No part of this book may be reproduced in any form or by any means without prior written permission from the holder of the copyright.

Olive Press, Leeuwerikstraat 4-b, 1021 GL Amsterdam.
www.olive-press.eu
info@olive-press.eu

Contents

Introduction..............................7

The Technique of Fresco Painting...............9
The Technique of Fresco Painting..............11
    Cartons................................14
    Mezzo Fresco..........................15
    Pigments..............................16
    Moving Murals.........................19

The Fresco Painter..........................21
    Working Conditions and Private Life..........23
    Talent................................29

Illustrations............................33-48

    Professional Pride.......................49
    Rivalry................................53
    Self-Portraits...........................57
    Originality.............................61
    Creative Idleness........................65

CONTENTS

Looking at Frescoes 69
    Narrative Painting 71
    Ambient Art 75
    Linear Perspective 81
    Naked Beauty 87
    Anatomist-Artist 93

Illustrations 97-112

    Body and Soul 113

Quoted Sources 119

Chronological Overview 121

Frescoes according to Region 133
    North West Italy 133
    North East Italy 134
    Lombardy and Emilia-Romagna 137
    Tuscany 140
    Umbria-Marches-Abruzzo-Molise 144
    Rome and Lazio 147
    Southern Italy 150

Maps 155

Introduction

Fresco painting, the application of watercolours to a layer of wet plaster, has for centuries been the most revered form of art in Italy. In this country, so endowed with artistic sensibility, fresco painting ranks in the top category of artistic disciplines. Almost all the great artists distinguished themselves as muralists. Giotto, Piero della Francesca, Raphael, Tiepolo, and many others, realised their principal works in fresco. Even Leonardo da Vinci, who seldom worked in the medium, and Michelangelo, who was by nature a sculptor, owe their fame to respectively the fresco of the *Last Supper* and the fresco paintings of the Sistine Chapel. For Cennino Cennini, who wrote an artist's handbook in c. 1400, fresco painting was 'the most pleasing and most beautiful work in existence'. In his introduction to his *Lives of the Artists (Le Vite,* 1550), Vasari called fresco art 'the most manly, most sure-handed and most durable of all methods. By age it continually acquires beauty and harmony in an infinitely greater degree than any of the others. This kind of painting cleans itself in the air, is proof against water, and always resists any blow.'

Thousands of frescoes from the 13th to the 18th century have been preserved. They offer an homogeneous impression of the development of a richly variegated art form that was practised according to strictly defined criteria. Most of the frescoes can still be seen in their original setting, so that today's visitors have little difficulty imagining themselves back in the time they were created. Even now Italian fresco paintings still enchant us with their astounding richness of style, their wonderful colours obtained from natural pigments, and the profundity and originality with which the age-old themes of western culture are depicted.

The Technique
of Fresco Painting

The Technique of Fresco Painting

A fresco (Italian: *affresco*, pl. *affreschi*) is a mural painted on a layer of wet plaster (fresco *intónaco*).

The painter Cennino Cennini gave an elaborate description of this technique in his *Artist's Handbook* (*Libro dell'arte*, c. 1400). In this he distinguishes the following stages:

1 *Arriccio*. The wall is first covered with a rough layer of mortar, the so-called *arriccio*. Its irregular surface provides a hold for the thin, smoother coat of mortar that is applied on top of this. The night and morning before the mortar is applied, the section of wall to be painted is dampened so that the mortar will remain fresh and moist throughout the day.
2 *Sinopia*. On the *arriccio*, the artist makes a charcoal sketch of the image he plans to paint. Once the charcoal sketch has been approved, he traces over it with an ochre paint thickened with *sinopia*, a reddish-brown earth pigment mixed with water. The name *sinopia* is derived from Sinope, a city on the shores of the Black Sea (in what is now Turkey) where the red earth from which the pigment was extracted was

imported from. Later, this pigmented sketch itself became known as the *sinopia* (pl 33-35).

3. *Intonaco.* When the *sinopia* is ready, it is covered bit by bit with a smooth layer of plaster known as the *intonaco.* Starting at the top and working down, the painter applies as much plaster as he thinks he can paint in one day. Any plaster that is unpainted at the end of the day is cut away with a knife. The painter Pontormo kept a precise record of his progress in his diary: '4th February [1555] I painted the head of the figure... On Sunday, 4th March, I painted the torso of the figure beneath his head, and on Monday the arm of the same figure, which is raised, as shown in this sketch... On Tuesday I painted the head belonging to the arm I mentioned...' These daily sections (*giornate*) are still visible in raking light. Where necessary, details can be added to the dry painting afterwards using the *a secco* (dry) technique. Cennini advised stirring the chalk plaster with a spatula until it had the consistency of ointment. Every artist had his own recipe for the preparation of the mortar, which is to consist of two parts of sand and one of lime and tiny variations in the mixture may offer a clue to the artist when attributing a fresco. Because the preparation and mixing of the plaster was such a specialised skill, the painter often left this toilsome task to an assistant or a professional plasterer, a *muratore*. Unslaked lime was a dangerous, caustic substance (it was strewn on corpses to speed up their decomposition and reduce the stench from graves, for instance). The lime was slaked with clear water in a covered trough and with so much water that there

may be a great excess above the lime. The *muratore* had to stir it well with the spade, kneading and working it thoroughly until the spade did not meet with any lumps or clods. The lime was not considered to be mature in less than three months. After mixing it with the sand, the *muratore* had to work it again and again with great labor until it almost froths. Only then the intonaco was ready to be applied to the *arriccio*. Some murals were realised partly or entirely *a secco*. Various complications with fresco painting could be avoided by working *a secco*. A painter working in the wet intonaco had to allow for the fact that the colours on the wet wall would dry up differently. But the migration of pigments absorbed by the plaster was an unpredictable process. A painting started in the morning could look different the next day. A rainy day could produce yet another effect. As a result, the painter would often be obliged to retouch his painting when it was dry using the *a secco* technique.

Another drawback to fresco painting was that the artist could not afford to make a mistake since the colours were instantly absorbed by the *intonaco*. Moreover, fresco painting demanded lengthy and laborious preparation.

The *a secco* technique offered advantages in all these respects. The painting surface was soon prepared. Once it was ready, the painter could work at his own pace, and any mistakes he made could easily be corrected. But the *a secco* technique had its drawbacks, too. It was less durable, since the paint could flake away when the binding agent became brittle. Also, the colours were less brilliant and tended to darken with age. Hence, *a secco* work was considered inferior to *buon fresco* painting, which was the preferred technique of dynamic, ambitious artists with the mettle to take on its challenges. A fresco painter was therefore known as an *amatore della difficoltà*, a lover of arduous, challenging projects.

Cartons

As the fresco progressed, the *sinopia* gradually disappeared beneath the finished painting. Painters were therefore required to memorise their sketch. They resolved this by sticking to fairly standard schemes. Thanks to the standardization of the work process the painter was able to recall non-standard details or to come back and add these at the last moment. In the course of the 15th century, however, painting evolved to such an extent that standard schemes no longer sufficed. Most painters then went over to using so-called *cartons* or cartoons, which consisted of sheets of paper glued together with a full-scale sketch of the finished fresco. The cartoon was a blow-up of a smaller sketch that was scaled up square by square by a process known as quadrating (pl. 36). This led to a division of labour. A master could concentrate on making the sketch and leave the quadrating to his pupils. Busy painters like Raphael or Vasari, who had to decorate vast surfaces in rapid tempo, embraced the new method. Vasari described this process as follows: 'When cartoons are used for frescoes or murals, a sheet of paper is cut to size and pressed against the wall, which should be freshly plastered and very smooth. This piece of cartoon is put in the place where the figure is to be painted. First a mark is made to show where to place the adjoining cartoon the next day. The artist then uses a stylus to transfer the outlines to the wall, engraving them in the fresh plaster, which yields to the pressure exercised on the paper, thereby leaving behind its imprint.'

Apart from using a stylus to trace the drawing on the cartoon on to the wet *intonaco*, the drawing could also be transferred by dusting charcoal through hundreds of tiny perforations of the cartoon's outlines (the *spolvero* technique). Ghirlandaio and Michelangelo transferred their cartoons to the *intonaco* using a combination of *spolvero* and incision techniques. Here, the finer details, such as faces and hair locks, were incised in the carton and transferred with a dusting of charcoal, while the outlines of bodies and clothing were traced with a stylus.

Mezzo fresco

In the 17th century the so-called *mezzo fresco* came into fashion. A painting in *mezzo fresco* was made in half-dry plaster. This meant that the pigments penetrated the stucco less deeply than when the plaster was freshly applied. Writing around 1700, the painter Andrea Pozzo (1642-1709) advised 'not to start painting until a finger hardly leaves an impression on the plaster.' He also advised 'granulating' the *intonaco* so the paint would stick to the fine grains of sand. The introduction of this technique went hand in hand with changes in the way frescoes were used. Frescoes were now mainly executed in large vaults or cupolas, and could only be viewed from a distance (pl 100). Hence, the artist used large, brushy strokes that could be seen from far off. This also enabled him to work faster, which was important in view of the vast surfaces that artists were required to cover. However, the transparency and luminosity that characterised the colours of *buon fresco* were largely lost. Often *mezzo fresco* applied to walls was subjected to an additional treatment to allow closer viewing. The rough surface was smoothed by covering the *intonaco* with paper and flattening the irregularities with a trowel.

Pigments

The brilliant colour palette is one of the most appealing aspects of fresco painting. Some pigments were extracted from the local soil (ochres, ombers, siennas); others were derived from plants (black from scorched vines or the seeds of fruit) or were of mineral origin or the product of simple chemical processes, as in the case of white lead. The pigments were ground in limewater and applied to the plaster. One brush was required for each colour. As they dried, the pigments were absorbed by the plaster, with which they fused to form a single substance. But not all pigments could be absorbed by wet plaster, the blues obtained from minerals, for instance, such as *lapis lazuli* (ultramarine) or *azurro d'Alemagna* (azurite). These pigments were therefore applied to a dry surface, *a secco*, with the help of a binding agent such as egg yolk or glue. Painters prepared their own pigments and binding agents. For some who sold them to colleagues this provided an additional source of income. The pigment stones were ground in nut-size chunks on a thick slab of red porphyry. For grinding the painter used a stone that was flat on one side but rounded on the other to fit in the palm of his hand. The colours were kept dust free under a layer of water in jars that were stored in a casket. Some mineral pigments, such as *hematite* (cardinal red) and *lapis lazuli*, were so hard they had to be pulverised in a bronze mortar, as they would have broken the porphyry slab. Some painters purchased their pigments from the monastery pharmacies. One of the reasons why the painters in Florence were members of the guild of physicians and pharmacists (*Arte dei Speziali e Medici*) was because many of the substances they bought as pigments and binding agents were also sold as medicines. Tragacanth gum, for example, was a common binding agent for pigments but was also an effective linctus for coughs and hoarseness. The blue pigment of *lapis lazuli* was useful in removing melancholy and was also given to children for disorders of the breast. The root of the madder plant produced a carmine red, but was also prescribed as a remedy for sciatica. The fresco painter Dario Varatori, who was undergoing medical treatment, took his medicine with him when working on the Basilica Santa Maria del Carmine in Padua. Disgusted by the taste after taking so much, he dipped his brush into it and used it to finish the drapery of one of the figures. Some painters went out into countryside to look for their own pigments. Cennini describes a trip he made with his father in search of pigments in the Colle di Val d'Elsa region of Tuscany. They came to a small, rugged valley. 'There I scraped the soil with a spade and I saw many veins of colour: ochre, dark and bright *sinopia*, blue and white. That white could be found in a vein in the soil was for me the greatest miracle in the world. There was even a vein of black soil. All these colours appeared in the soil exactly like a wrinkle in a person's face. I scraped the colour out of the wrinkle with a knife and never had I seen a more beautiful ochre.'

Cennini mentions the following pigments:

- *Terra di Siena* was an iron-rich clay from the hills around Siena that gave a yellowish brown colour. When heated it produced a red-brown pigment known as burnt sienna.
- *Terra verde pigment* was made from a grey-green mineral (glauconite) that was found in the vicinity of Verona.
- *Bianco sangiovanni*, a white pigment from Florence, was obtained by keeping slaked lime in a pit for weeks until a thick paste had formed which was then exposed to the sun to solidify.
- *Ivory black*, a pigment derived from charred ivory. It was often used for the depiction of hair. Black was also made from stones, scorched vines or the burnt kernels of almonds or peaches.
- *Smalt* (*smaltino*, glass blue) is a pigment obtained by grinding glass tinted with blue cobalt. Its production was a specialism of the Gesuati monks of the San Giusto alle Mura Monastery near Florence. The monastery was known throughout Europe for its production of stained glass. The monks heated the cobalt ore in an oven (*smaltino* meaning 'molten') and mixed the resulting cobalt oxide with molten glass. The tinted glass was then ground into a pigment.
- *Ultramarine* (*azzurro oltramarino*) was a blue shipped in from overseas. It was made from *lapis lazuli* quarried in Afghanistan and imported via the port of Venice. Ultramarine was applied *a secco* with a binding agent in the same manner as mineral pigments such as azzurite, vermillion and malachite. *Lapis lazuli* was very expensive and its preparation extremely labour-intensive. One had to break the stone in a bronze

mortar and then grind it endlessly with clear water. Fearing it might be stolen, the painter Perugino was protected by guards when he used ultramarine in the frescoes of the corridors of the cloister of San Giusto alle Mura. Sometimes even the blues on frescoes have been scraped off for the value of the ultramarine. The authorities also checked whether painters did not secretly use the much cheaper azzurite, a form of fraud that was punishable by the guilds of Florence, Siena and Perugia.

Moving murals

When frescoes have to be moved to another support, they are removed from the wall in the following manner. First a cotton fabric is glued to them with an elastic adhesive to protect them. The fabric prevents the *intonaco* from cracking or falling when it is lifted off the wall. A wooden frame is constructed on the wall around the painting. The fabric overlapping the edges of the painting is nailed to the frame. Working from the bottom up, with the help of metal levers, the painted stucco is chipped off the wall bit by bit. The painting is then reassembled face down on a flat surface. Next, the thin layer of painted stucco is mounted on a new support, usually a fibre plate. The painting is then turned over painted side up. The cotton fabric that was glued to the surface of the painting can then be removed.

Another method involves a glue that when dry is stronger than the original plaster of the mural. Once again protective cloth is glued to the painting, the upper edge of which is nailed to the wall with a slat. The plaster a few millimetres beneath the painting is then chiselled away. When the cloth is dry the fresco is lifted away from the wall and rolled up. In the laboratory the fresco is rolled out on a table, painted side down. The rest of the procedure is as for the first method. In Vasari's day, and possibly even earlier, frescoes also occasionally had to be moved. This was a mammoth undertaking which involved cutting away whole sections of wall. When the choir was renovated in the Ognissanti church in Florence, the frescoes of St. Jerome and St. Augustine by Ghirlandaio and Botticelli, respectively, were carefully cut away, and, attached to slats with iron strips, moved to the nave where they can still be found today.

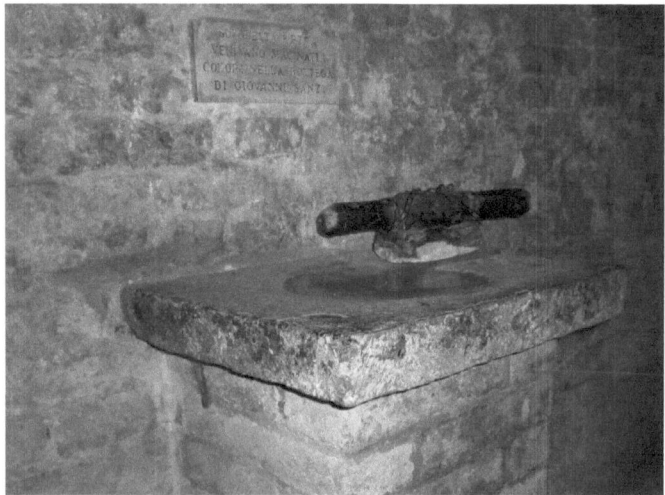

Table and stone for grinding pigments

The Fresco Painter

Working Conditions and Private Life

Besides being an artist, a master fresco painter was also the manager of a studio and a team of pupils and assistants. The composition of the team and the studio location varied according to the assignment. Since frescoes were made to order in situ, the term studio also came to refer to the team working on the assignment. While lifelong partnerships did occur, teams tended to be formed around the assignment and a collaboration lasted as long as it took to complete the work, which in turn depended on the size of the assignment. Sometimes an assistant executed a commission on his own. In such cases, it was customary for him to pay the master a third of the fee. It was also not uncommon for several independent masters to agree to work together on an assignment. Finally, there were the specialists who were hired for specific parts of the painting. Some might specialise in *grotesques* (Giovanni da Udine, Raphael's assistant, pl. p. 109 below), while others (like Mengozzi Colonna, the lifelong partner of Giambattista Tiepolo (1696-1770) (pl. p. 111) confined themselves to the architectonic details of the design (*quadratura*).

Whatever the case, the execution of a fresco was never the work of one man alone. Some form of cooperation was inevitable, particularly when creating a complete cycle of frescoes. This was a complex undertaking that required a great deal of organising and preparation before the actual painting could start: the design had to be devised, sketched and then upscaled, the colours prepared, the plaster applied, and the wall made ready for painting. Some four to six men would be at work on the scaffold at one time, amid troves, pots of watercolours, buckets, brushes, sacks of sand and limestone.

Fresco painting was heavy work. Fortunately, the true fresco painter in Italy was an acknowledged *amatore della difficoltà,* a lover of challenges. He welcomed projects that tested his talent and temperament. And they were indeed put to the test: painters had to work for hours in awkward positions, standing on a scaffold painting a vault above their heads. Some painters constructed chairs with a folding back like a dental chair for painting vaults and cupolas, but even then it was never easy. Despite the discomfort, painters preferred to work non-stop, without taking a break, to take full advantage of the wet plaster. For it was hard enough work applying the plaster. Often a painter began to work at sunrise and used to persevere at his work until dusk, because, in the words of the painter Matteo Rosselli, he wished to leave the intonaco, and not the intonaco to leave him. The proverbial Italian lunch was usually sacrificed. Rather than climbing up and down the scaffold, painters chose to take wine and bread up with them and ate as they worked, a crust of bread in one hand, a paintbrush in the other. Luca Giordano thought even that too time-consuming and had his father feed him while he painted so he could go on working. When a fresco painter took on a commission outside his home town, as was often the case, the whole team would move into some shabby accommodation together for months. This was an all-male household and there were no home comforts. Even a celebrity like Michelangelo had to be content with a ramshackle studio in a noisy alley by the city wall in the *Borgo dei Angeli* neighbourhood in the years he worked on the vault of the Sistine Chapel. Michelangelo was probably not exaggerating when he said: 'However rich I may have been, I have always lived like a pauper.' Other artists hired a woman to live in and do the housekeeping and cooking. She regularly doubled as a model or concubine or both. At times this blossomed into a serious relationship. Raphael was so fond of his model and mistress that he refused to work on the Villa Farnesina unless his patron Agostini Chigi allowed her to accompany him. She posed for the painting known as *La Fornarina* in the Palazzo Barberini in Rome and may well have modelled for some of the women painted in the loggia of the Villa Farnesina.

There were many hilarious anecdotes in circulation about the Bohemian lifestyle in artists' studios. But the harsh working and living conditions coupled with being cooped up together day and night caused tension which regularly escalated into violent rows. Hence, it was a great advantage if a painter was easy-going by nature and could get along well with people. Raphael was such a person. He is said to have been like a father to his pupils and assistants. He was amiable and always willing to help. Others, though, had more difficulty combining their artistry with management. Michelangelo and Leonardo were notorious examples of artists who looked upon their co-workers as a necessary evil. They preferred to send them home so they could be alone. Leonardo was adamant that a painter should not have to bother about everyday matters and should avoid people who distracted him from his art. He wrote: 'When you are alone, you are your own master, whereas in company you are only half yourself, or even less, depending on how discrete the others are. And even if you say, "I won't take any notice of the others, I'll study," I promise you, you won't be able to stop yourself from listening to their chatter.' Sexual desire he curbed with spiritual weapons. For 'the passion of the spirit expels the charm of the senses'.

Pontormo also preferred his own company (p. 28). He could not bear people to watch him and he shut himself away, for years even, in the chapel where he was working. When he got back to his attic room, he would pull up the ladder so as not to be disturbed and avoid unwanted visitors. In the latter years of his life, he kept a diary which testifies to his intense introspection; every shift in his physical and mental make-up was promptly recorded. Completing Pontormo's psychological profile, Vasari tells us that he was incredibly solitary, lived virtually all his life alone, and refused to let anyone help him or cook for him. He was so afraid of death he forbade anyone to mention it. He never attended festivities or other events. And what people disliked most about him was that he was only willing to paint if he felt in the mood, for someone he liked, and then only how he wanted.

Given the working conditions and the specific demands of the profession, it is not surprising that few fresco artists enjoyed a normal married life. Art and marriage did not go well together. Michelangelo, Leonardo da Vinci, Raphael, Botticelli, Piero di Cosimo and many others all remained single, irrespective of their sexual preference.

When a priest complained to Michelangelo about his bachelor status – which meant that he could not bequeath the fruits of his labour to his children – the artist declared that his art was already one wife too many and that he regarded his works as his children. Michelangelo's response no doubt summed up the feelings of most of his colleagues: the profession was so exacting, it demanded the artist's complete and utter dedication.

28 WORKING CONDITIONS AND PRIVATE LIFE

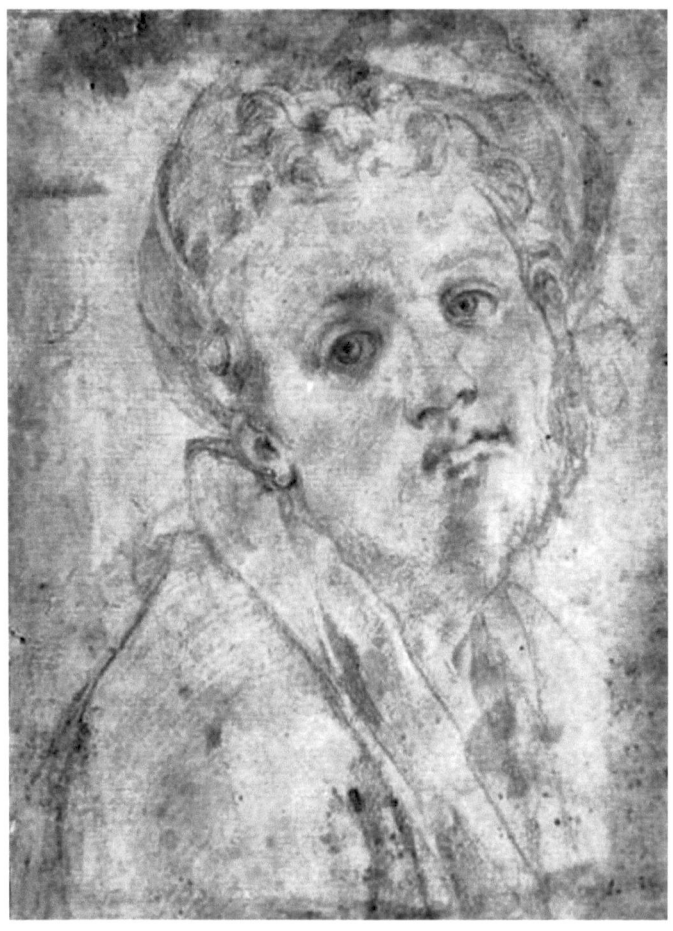

Pontormo (1494-1557, Self-portrait

Talent

A proficient fresco painter can be recognized by his flair and his fast and decisive way of working. Italians used the term *facilità* for this. Related notions are *sprezzatura* (complete effortlessness) and *prompto* (resolute, decisive).

A fresco painter had no choice but to work quickly without making mistakes. For he always had a deadline to meet, namely, the moment the plaster was dry (see *The technique of fresco painting*). Since the plaster instantly absorbed the colours, every brushstroke was irrevocable. No corrections could be made. Therefore, fresco painting required both quickness and facility of execution.

A skilled painter maintained his *facilità* under all circumstances, even when painting ambitious fresco cycles. No matter how many difficulties he encountered, he seemed to take the challenges that art presented in his stride. Some artists made quite a show of the *facilità* with which they painted. Lorenzo di Bicci executed his work in the convent of Santa Croce, Florence, with so much quickness and facility that once when he was sent for by a monk who used to procure his dinner just as he had laid on the intonaco for a figure, and begun to paint, he said, 'Put on the saucepans, for I will just finish this figure, and then I will come.' Amico Aspertini (c. 1474-1552) also boasted an astounding work tempo. In a chapel in the San Frediano in Lucca he painted the frescoes of the history of the *Volto Santo* using two brushes simultaneously so as to waste no time, painting non-stop with one hand, while plunging the brush in the other into the paint. Round his waist he bound a leather strap, to which hung his gallipots of tempered colours. Over a century later the Neapolitan painter Luca Giordano (1634-1705) worked as if his life depended on it. Countless nicknames allude to the speed he worked at: 'Luca Fà-Presto ('Speedy Luca'), 'Proteus', or 'Il Fulmine' ('The Thunderbolt').

This fast, almost effortless way of working was regarded as an irrefutable sign of talent. Just as some people can pick out a thoroughbred horse by its trot, others can identify a master from a single pencil stroke. A well-known tale from antiquity has it that Protagenes had only to see a single line to recognise the hand of Apelles. Likewise, Vasari relates how, when the pope asked for proof of Giotto's mastership, he drew a perfect circle with a brush in the presence of the papal nuncio. He then handed the drawing to the perplexed envoy. The moral of the story is that one should not judge a painting by the time invested in it, but by the talent and craftsmanship reflected in the handwriting. However hard a mediocre painter tries, he can never match the *facilità*, the effortlessness and faultlessness, of his more talented colleague.

Facilità should not be confused with slap-dashness. The paradox of *facilità* is that it is extremely difficult to do things effortlessly and it takes a great deal of discipline. It is not just a matter of the number of hours that are put in. The painter has to use his intelligence, and know when to tighten the rein and when to relax it. Artists were advised to stop working and turn their mind to something else as soon as they noticed they had less pleasure in their work and were becoming mentally stale and less focused. It was this that prompted the art theoretician Alberti to advise aspiring painters to work briefly but intensely under the motto *Diligenza con prestezza* (diligence with speed).

The high esteem of fresco painting in Italy may have been partly responsible for the promotion of the *facilità* required in fresco painting to a general artistic principle, a way of life even. It was considered undignified and a sign of spiritual impoverishment to be excessively zealous and over-diligent. In the *Book of the Courtier* (*Il Cortegiano*), a 16th century bestseller on *savoir-vivre*, Baldassare Castiglione writes: 'We have a natural admiration for a man who seems carefree and who shows ease and naturalness in all that he says and does. It would seem there is more to him than meets the eye and that but the tip of the veil has been lifted on his abilities.' On the other hand, he should not flaunt it. That would make him artificial, 'for some people pretend to be so easy-going that they clearly make a lot of effort to be without worry and so they worry too much'.

Though hard to define, contemporaries claimed they were somehow able to see from a completed painting the effortlessless with which it had been made. Murals painted at speed had a certain indefinable grace, and a fluid, richly modulated rhythm both in the work as a whole and in the detailing. Irrespective of their diversity and complexity, the scenes radiated a natural grace as if they could not have been painted in any other way. 'For art truly mastered, does not convey the impression of art' was a much-heard saying, as was 'Art lies in concealing art'. The aim then was to convey the impression that the fresco had been no effort to paint, as if it had been produced with a simple wave of the brush.

Excessive effort, too much precision and incessant study, on the other hand, were said to result in a vigourless and barren style. As a warning, Vasari quoted the example of the painter Paolo Uccello (1387-1475) who had studied linear perspective so intensively that he had exhausted his vital powers. His talent became stale and he grew depressed and eccentric. This was reflected in his work, which lost all freshness and spontaneity. Sebastiano del Piombo (c. 1485-1547) was a similar case. According to Vasari, he went to enormous lengths with all his art and that took all the pleasure out of his work. He felt discouraged knowing that his colleague Salviati could paint something in a few hours that would take him days to produce. When the pope offered him an easy job, Sebastiano del Piombo was only too glad to give up his painting career. He admitted that he did not want to work anymore, 'because there are painters today who can complete a work in two months which would take me two years.' For if a painter has no talent, he will never acquire the *facilità*, the capacity to produce *virtuoso* work at speed.

THE TECHNIQUE OF FRESCO PAINTING

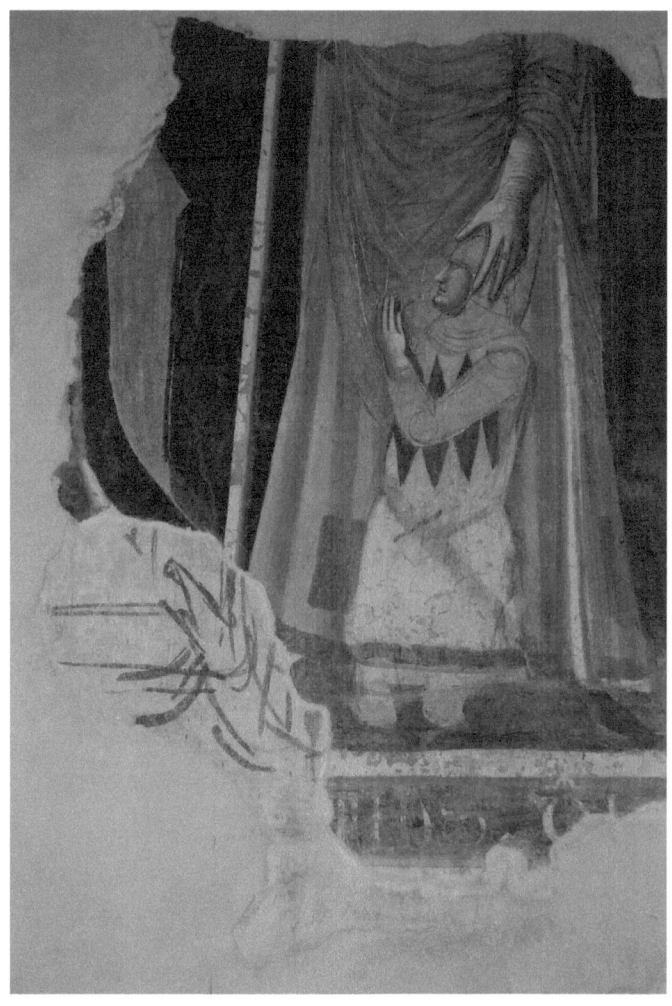

Detail of a fresco with the sinopia partly visible

34 TECHNIQUE OF FRESCO PAINTING

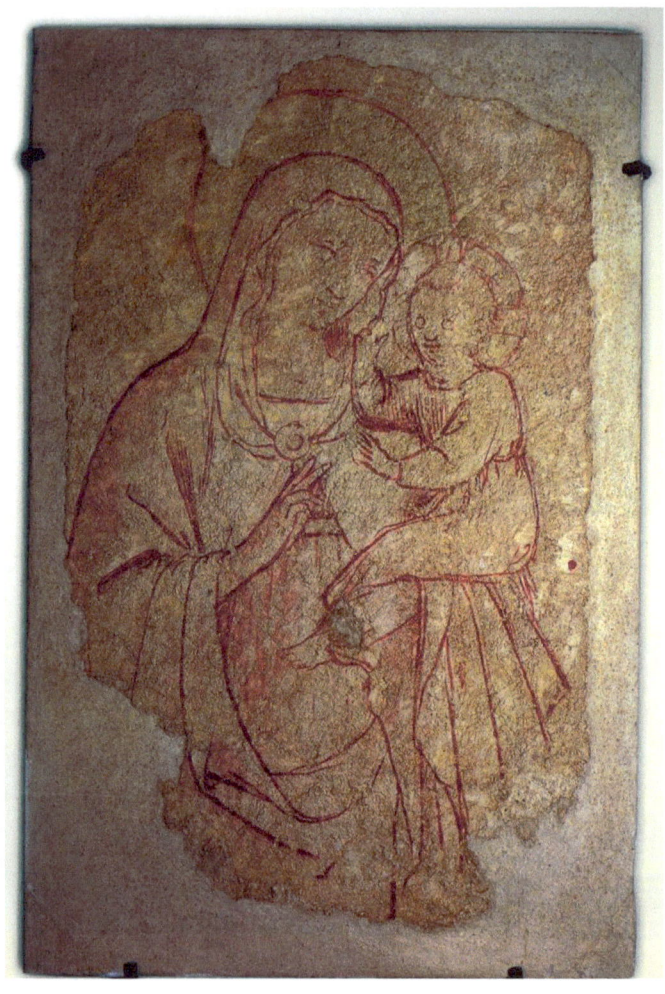

This and next page: Sinopia and fresco of *Madonna and Child*

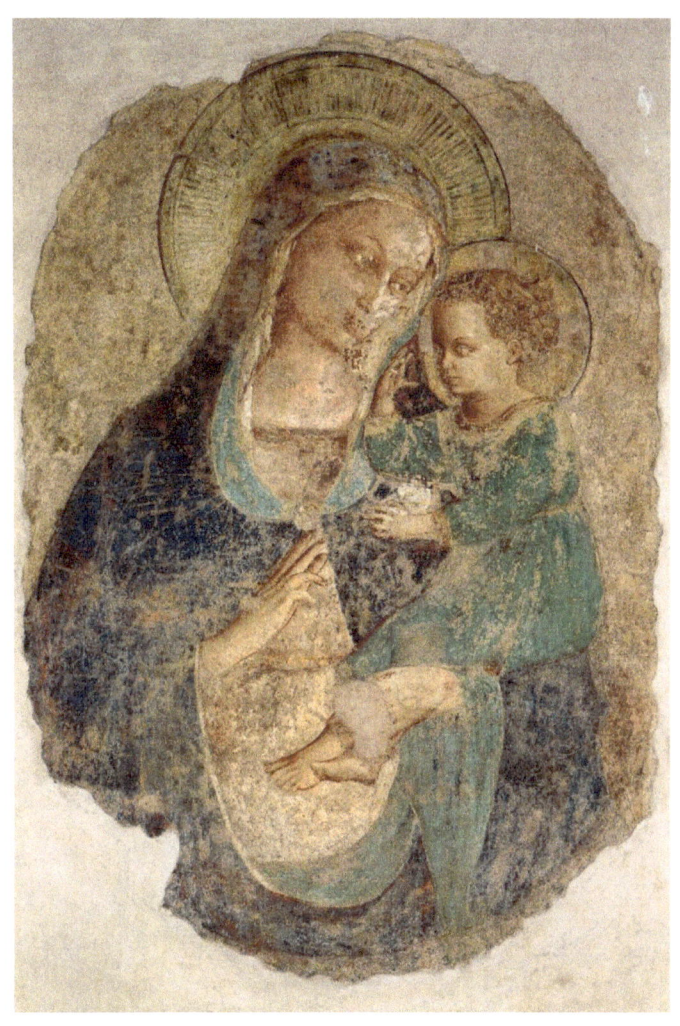

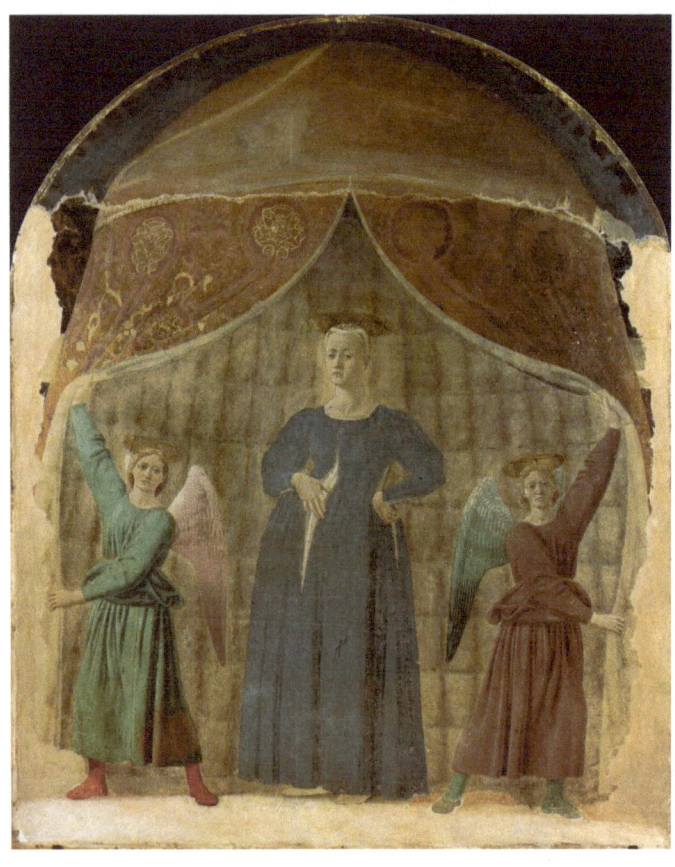

Piero della Francesca, *Madonna del Parto*, Monterchi; the two angels were realised by the artist with the same cartoon

SELF-PORTRAITS

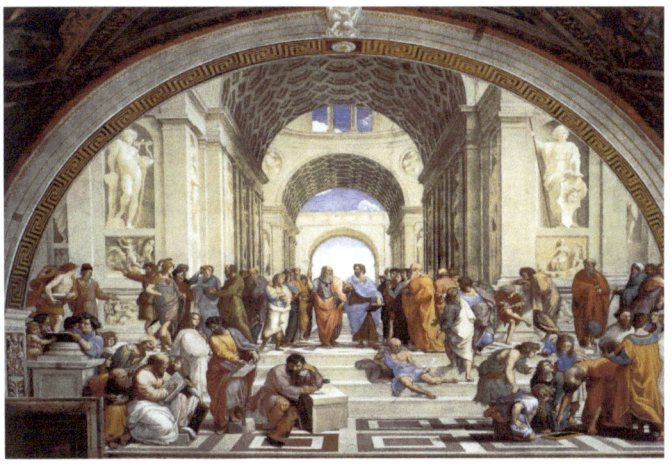

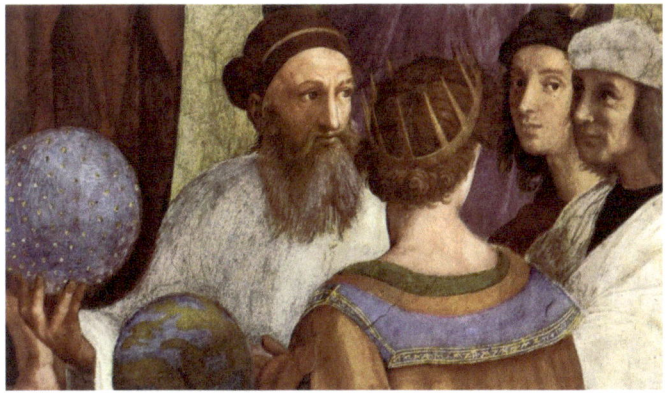

Above: Raphael, *School of Athens*, 1509, Stanza della Segnatura, Vatican

Below: Detail with a self-portrait and portrait of Il Sodoma, next to Zoroaster and Ptolemy

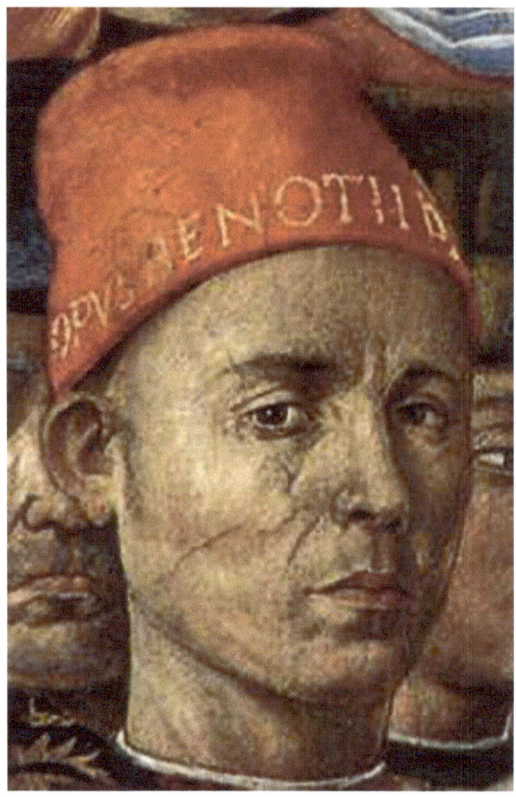

Benozzo Gozzoli, Self-portrait, *detail of the Journey of the Magi,* c. 1460, Palazzo Medici-Riccardi, Florence

Next page, above: Pinturicchio, Self-portrait, detail of the *Annunciation*, Santa Maria Maggiore, Spello

below: Domenico Ghirlandaio, *Expulsion of Joachim from the temple*, detail with self-portrait and portraits of assistants

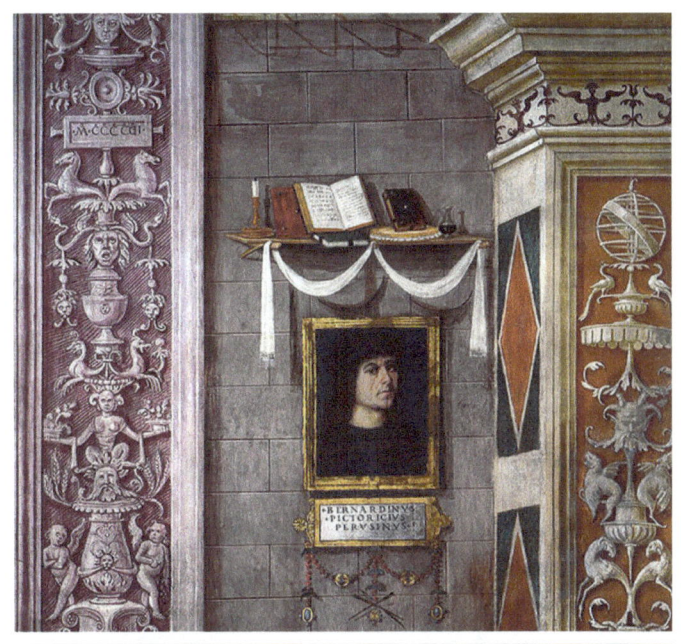
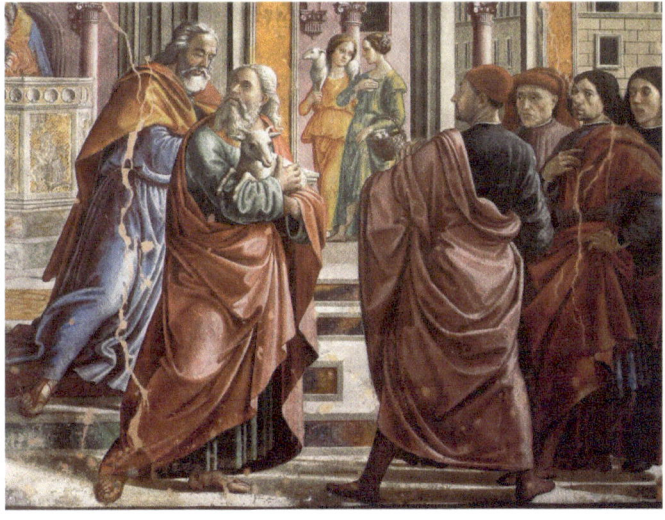

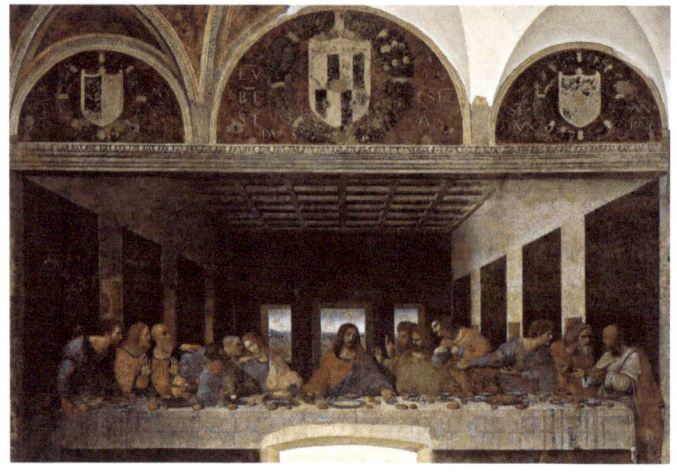

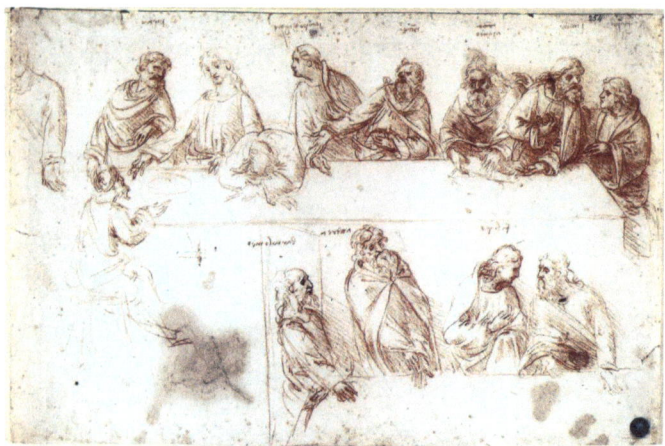

Above: Leonardo da Vinci, *Last Supper*, 1494-1498, Santa Maria delle Grazie, Milan

Below: Study of composition of the *Last Supper*

NARRATIVE PAINTING

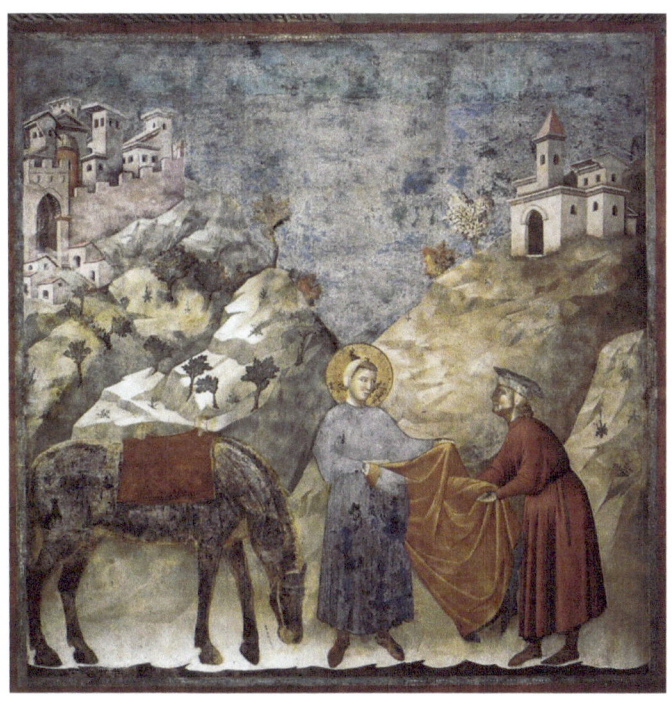

Giotto, *St. Francis giving his mantle to a poor man*, 1297-1299, San Francesco, Upper Church, Assisi

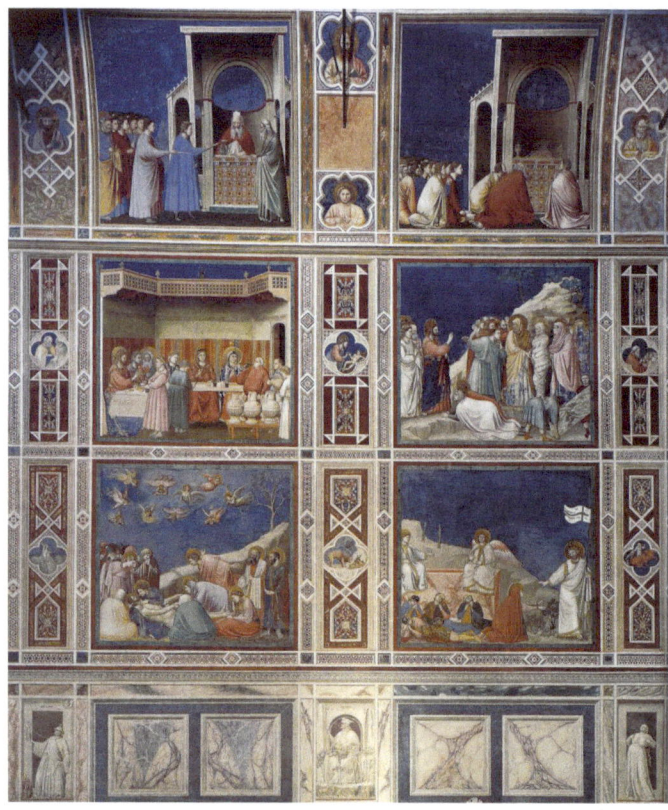

Giotto, c. 1305, Scrovegni Chapel, Padua

NARRATIVE PAINTING 43

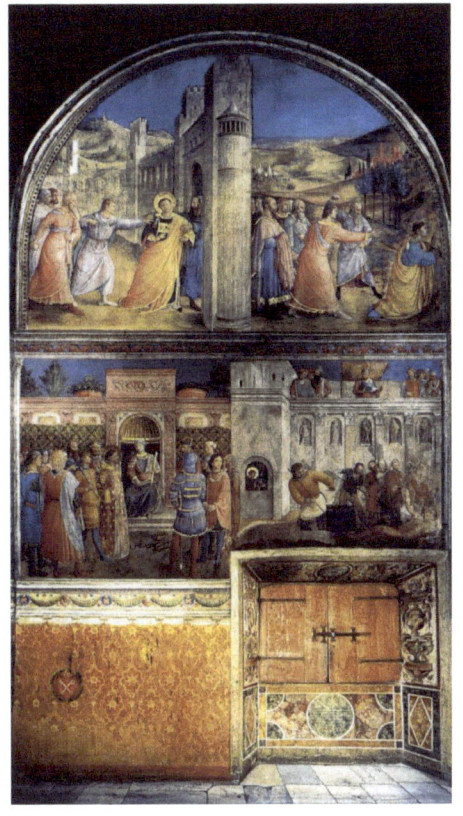

Fra Angelico, 1447-1451, Chapel of Nicolas V, Vatican

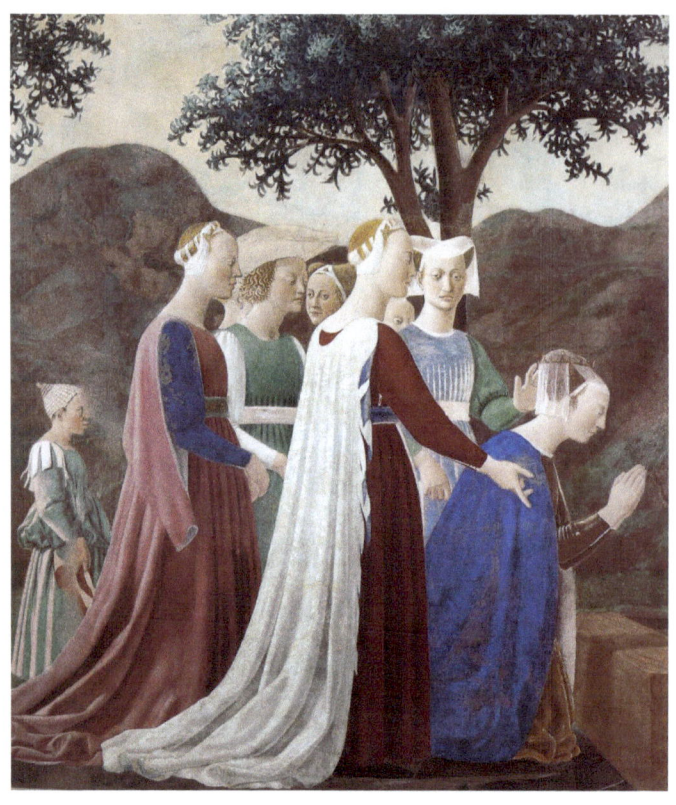

Piero della Francesca, 1452-1466, *The Queen of Sheba* (detail), San Francesco, Arezzo

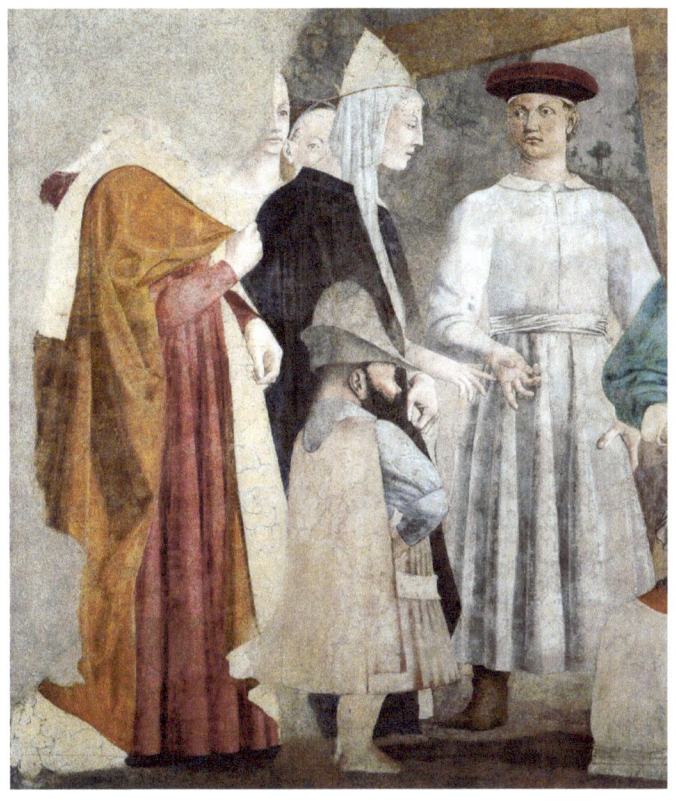

Piero della Francesca, 1452-1466, *St. Helena* (detail), San Francesco, Arezzo

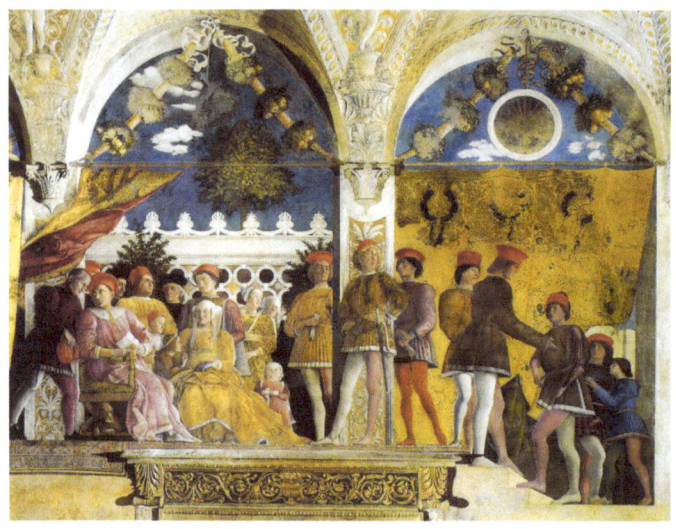

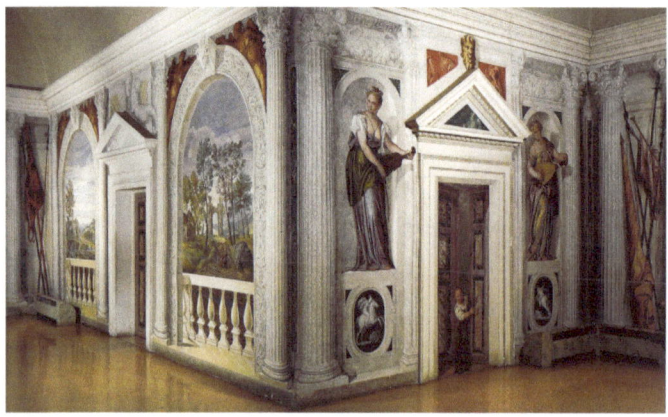

Above: Andrea Mantegna, *The court of Gonzaga*, 1465-1474, Camera degli Sposi, Palazzo Ducale, Mantua.

Below: Paolo Veronese, c. 1560, *Villa Barbaro*, Maser

AMBIENT ART 47

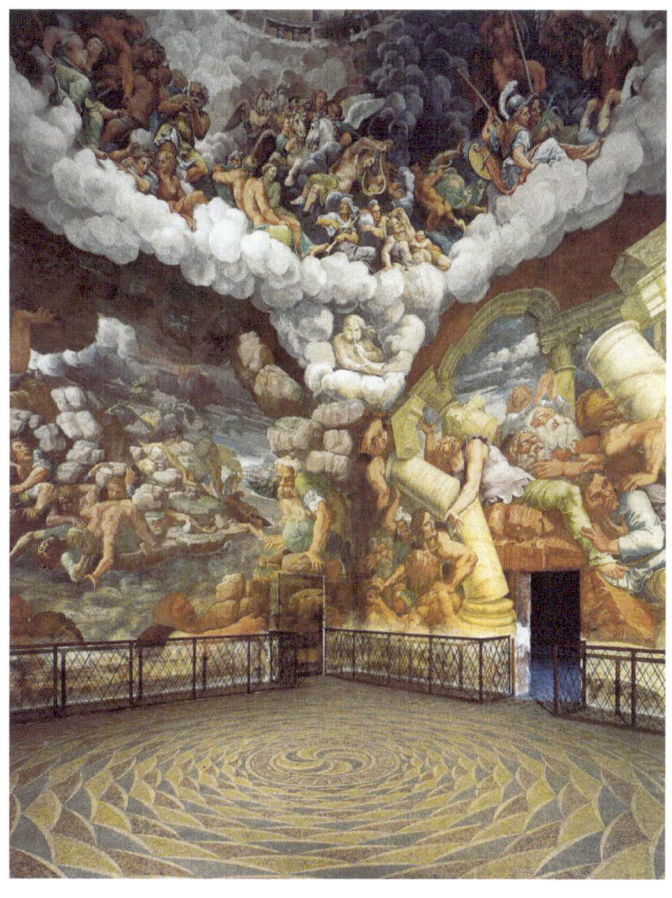

Giulio Romano, *Sala dei Giganti*, c. 1530, Palazzo del Te, Mantua

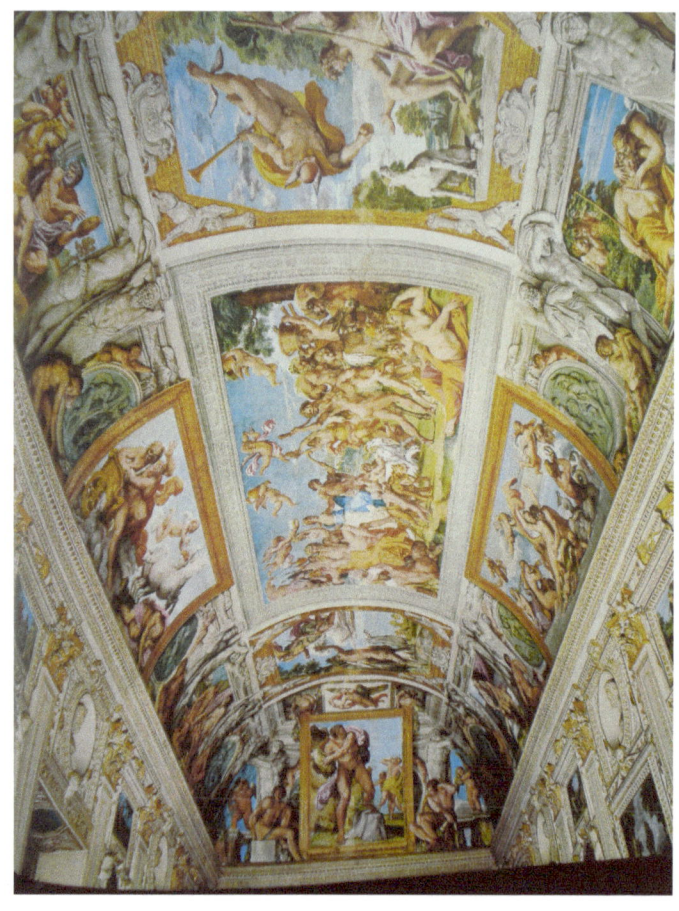

Annibale Carracci, Ceiling fresco, 1597-1602, Palazzo Farnese, Rome

Professional Pride

It was in the nature of Renaissance culture to cultivate inflated egos, certainly among painters. Their ambition was fuelled by their belief that painting was underrated compared with other disciplines. Painting had a low status in the Middle Ages. It was considered a craft and as such was not classed with the higher ranking liberal arts (*artes liberales*). This was a thorn in the eye of professional painters. Painting was so much more than just mixing colours and wielding a brush proficiently. Like other liberal arts, painting required theoretical knowledge and intellect, and above all creativity and imagination. At the very least, a painter needed a basic knowledge of all the science and humanities subjects on the curriculum of the liberal arts. He had to be well versed in both the Bible and classical mythology, and have a certain historical awareness as well as a considerable knowledge of geometry, optics, anatomy and poetry. What is more, their experiments with perspective and anatomy added considerable weight to their claim to a place among the liberal arts.

From an early date, painters in Italy had found an ally in influential poets. Boccaccio admired Giotto because he had restored painting to its former glory after it had been perverted for centuries by the incompetence of artists who had painted for the eyes of the ignorant rather than the minds of the wise. According to Boccaccio, Giotto was so gifted that anything he depicted, whether in pencil, pen or brush, was so lifelike that those who saw it were deluded into mistaking the representation for the real thing. Petrarch was equally sympathetic to painting as Boccaccio and he too had a favourite painter, Simone Martini, with whom he was very close. In their admiration for painters, the poets perpetuated the tradition of the classical writers who regarded painting and poetry as sister arts. Aristotle had already noted that poets can paint images of nature in their mind's eye in the same way a painter does on canvas. '*Ut pictura poesis*,' Horace wrote in his *Ars Poetica (The Art of Poetry)*: 'as is painting so is poetry'. A variation on this theme was the dictum coined by Plutarch: '*Poema pictura loquens, pictura poema silens*', 'a poem is a speaking painting, a painting a silent poem'. Horace insisted that poets and painters should have the artistic licence to follow their imagination, provided they did not compromise their credibility. Another similarity Horace observed between the two art forms was that just as some paintings should be viewed from close by and others from a distance, some poems lend themselves to slow, close reading whereas others do not.

Despite the generally ambiguous attitude to the visual arts in antiquity, it was common belief in the Renaissance that painting enjoyed a high standing in this classical era. Contemporaries bore this out by repeating the same anecdotes about the special relationship between Alexander the Great and his court painter Apelles. Alexander (the greatest ruler of his time) so admired Apelles (the most talented painter of his day) that he offered him his concubine, Campasme, with whom the painter had fallen in love. Tales like this were a valuable propaganda instrument for reminding ambitious rulers and dignitaries of the obligation their position brought to patronise the visual arts.

In Italy such ideas did indeed become widely adopted. In his standard work on etiquette, *The Book of the Courtier* (1528), Castiglione declares that a courtier should be able to hold an interesting conversation on painting. This would imply that painting was regarded as an inalienable component of a particular lifestyle. Painting had high snob appeal. The social pressure to score in this area can be inferred from a statement by Michelangelo that Francisco da Holanda recorded: 'Talented painters only deem a few minds worthy of their painting. Only the high-minded are able to understand art. He who neither understands nor appreciates painting should reproach himself and not the art, which is of noble and high origins. Such a person is a barbarian, bereft of understanding.' Michelangelo, like Leonardo and Raphael, stood at the end of a developmental process that had begun two centuries before, in the days of Giotto. Painters had emancipated themselves from being nameless craftsmen to named artists, who, once successful, enjoyed unrivalled celebrity status. The latter came with high salaries and honoured positions bestowed on them by people of the highest standing. In 1555 this emancipatory movement resulted in the founding of the first official academy of art in Florence under the aegis of Giorgio Vasari. Other countries followed suit, and the art academy subsequently evolved into the artistic equivalent of a university. The notion of painting as a 'higher' art form had finally triumphed.

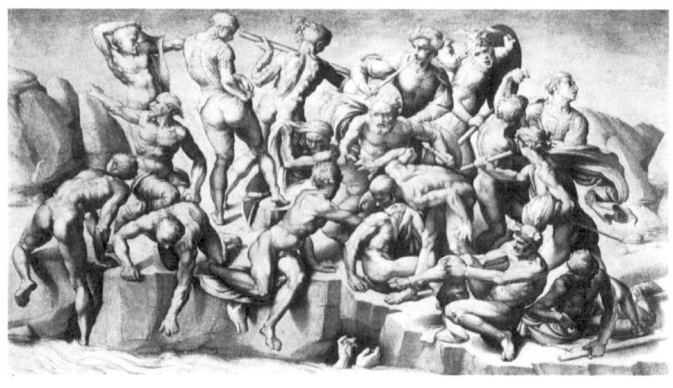

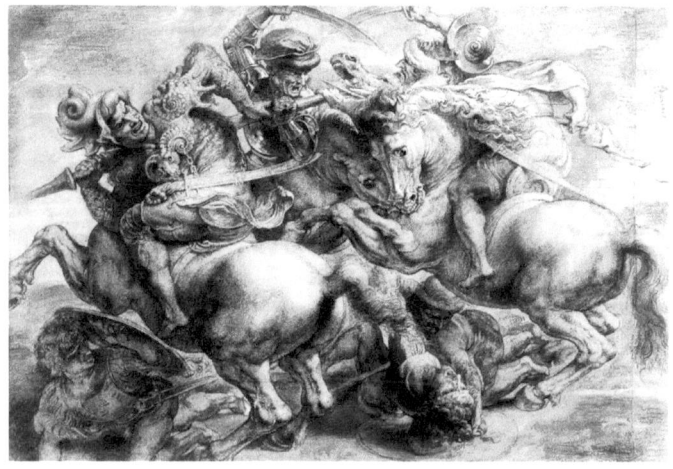

Above: engraving after Michelangelo's cartoon of the *Battle of Cascina*

Below: Peter Paul Rubens, drawing after Leonardo da Vinci's cartoon of the *Battle of Anghiari*

Rivalry

Painters were always ready to take to the barricades if their professional pride was at stake. But their solidarity ended there. The competition among the painters was cut-throat and they spared no-one to get ahead and rise to fame. There are many instances of painters tricking their rivals and stealing each other's assignments. Elbowing their way up was partly a way of surviving and partly a matter of pride. Personal pride played an important part in Italy, where the painter's individual artistry was highly valued. According to Vasari, it was this competitive attitude that paved the way for the rapid succession of spectacular innovations that hallmarked painting in this period. Rivalry was further stimulated by the contests that were organised for major projects or by hiring several masters to work on the same assignment. The most important assignments were usually frescoes, either in churches, town halls or other public spaces that attracted large crowds. The confrontation between Leonardo da Vinci and Michelangelo, two artists who differed in every possible respect, in the early 16th century was legendary. Both were asked to complete a vast fresco depicting glorious battle scenes from Florentine history on the walls of the main hall of the

Palazzo Vecchio, the town hall in Florence. Leonardo da Vinci was to paint the *Battle of Anghiari*, Michelangelo the *Battle of Cascina*, similar motifs which meant they could be compared. For various reasons, neither artist got any further than the full-scale design on the cartoons. But that was enough to attract hordes of admirers for years to come and to compare the two masterpieces. They were clearly showpieces in which the one endeavoured to outstrip the other by showing what they were capable of. They instinctively concentrated on the qualities they excelled in most. Michelangelo went all out with his knowledge of the human body, portraying it in great detail in unusual postures. Leonardo demonstrated his mastery in depicting horses and facial expressions.

But artistic talent alone was no guarantee for success, and artists occasionally resorted to ruthless methods to topple their adversaries. In 17th-century Naples, the leading painters formed a Cabal to stifle outside competition. Foreign artists who dared to encroach on their territory fell prey to the notorious mafia practices of corruption, sabotage, intrigue and poison. One of their victims was the Bolognese painter Domenico Zampieri (1581-1641), whose small stature earned him the name of Il Domenichino. In 1629 he was commissioned to decorate the Cappella del Tesoro in the cathedral, Naples' holiest shrine, where the skull and blood of the city patron, San Gennaro, were kept. Initially, the chapel had been painted by local artists. But the patron had not been satisfied with their work, and had ordered the paintings to be removed and invited painters from Bologna, who had a high reputation as superb fresco painters, to redo them. All of them awaited the same hostile reception in Naples. One by one they left the city, including Guido Reni, whose servant had been assaulted on leaving the house. Then it was Domenichino's turn to grapple with the Cabal of Naples. Shortly after his arrival, he received a death threat warning him to abandon the commission. Domenichino would often arrive at the chapel to find his previous day's work had been effaced. When he unveiled the first part of his painted decorations, the local painters got their friends to mingle with the public and spread criticism and disparaging remarks about Domenichino's work. The Neapolitan painters went so far as to get the mason of the building to mix ash in the lime of the plaster so the paint would flake off straight away. In the end, even his servants and his son-in-law sided with the rival painters, conspiring to bring about his ruin to make his daughter the sole heir on his death. Consumed with constant fear and suspicion, Domenichino died on 15 April 1641. His widow was convinced he had been poisoned by the Cabal. In the cathedral where he had painted in the hope of fame and reward, his body was entombed with no further pomp or circumstance.

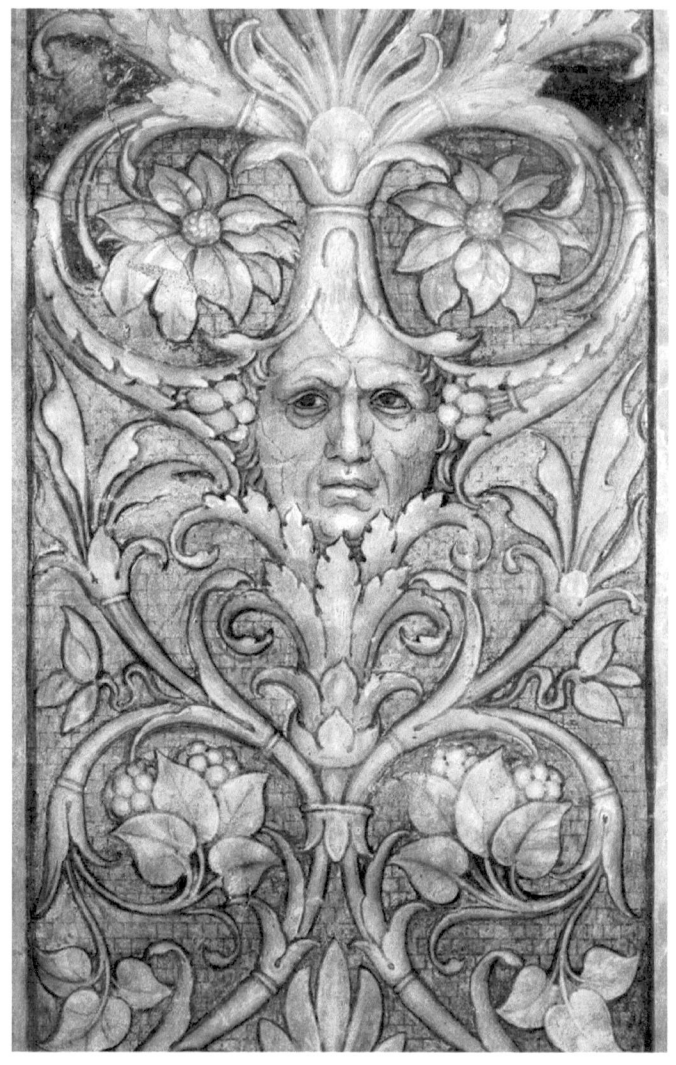

Andrea Mantegna, Self-portrait hidden in the foliage next to the door of the *Sala degli Sposi,* Palazzo Ducale, Mantua

Self-Portraits

Many renaissance frescoes feature a self-portrait of the painter, either on his own or in the company of his assistants. It was no doubt included with the consent, or even at the request, of the patron. Patrons were proud to have been able to enlist the services of a particular painter and it was their way of showing this. For the artist, for his part, incorporating a self-portrait was a good opportunity to promote his work. A self-portrait acted therefore as a business card. Generally speaking, portraiture is the most traditional painting genre, so that when a painter opted for a self-portrait he endeavoured to create something special.

Two examples from the 15th century illustrate this. Benozzo Gozzoli (1420-1497) depicted himself twice in the frescoes of *The Journey of the Magi* in the chapel of the Palazzo Medici-Riccardi in Florence (pl. p. 38). Whether by choice or request, he was not so immodest as to portray himself ostentatiously. In one instance, he is merely one of the courtiers in the retinue of the young king; in the other, he stands half-hidden behind a horse in the painting of the elder king. And yet, both portraits must have attracted attention. In the painting of the young king he is the only one who can be identified, the inscription *ben noti* (well noted) visible on the band of his cap being an ingenious wordplay on his own name Benozzo Gozzoli. On the opposite wall, in the scene of the elder king, he uses another novelty. There he raises his right hand, one of enormous proportions, indicating that he had personally created these fine paintings with his own hand. Domenico Ghirlandaio (1449-1494) likewise frequently appears in the many fresco cycles he produced in the course of his career. He can be recognised as the one pointing proudly at himself so that there can be no mistaking who created the paintings. He appears in this manner in the fresco of the *Expulsion of Joachim from the Temple* in the Tornabuoni Chapel of the Santa Maria Novella in Florence (pl. p. 39 below). He and his assistants form a group of four on the right-hand side of the composition. On the facing wall, a group of four well-known contemporary scholars similarly figures in *The Angel appears before Zacharias*. Was this arrangement a conscious allusion to the equal standing of painting and the traditional liberal arts? In the fresco *The School of Athens* in the *Stanze della Segnatura* in the Vatican, Raphael portrayed himself and his colleague Il Sodoma among the group of philosophers on the right-hand side of the composition, as if he was delighted to be one of the intellectual elite of classical antiquity (pl. p. 39). In the same painting he painted Plato with the features of Leonardo da Vinci and Heraclitus with those of Michelangelo. By identifying artists with classical philosophers Raphael emphasized the intellectual status painters had acquired in the Renaissance.

Finally, Pinturicchio (c.1454-1515) was another artist with a well-developed instinct for public relations. His pseudonym Pinturicchio (the 'Rich Painter'; his real name was Bernardo di Betto) betrays his ambition to climb the social ladder. In the Baglioni Chapel in Spello he painted a remarkable gold-framed self portrait on canvas as part of the fresco on the wall to the right of the fresco of the *Annunciation* (pl. p 39 above). A fine Latin inscription on a cartouche beneath the painting bears his name: Pictorisius Perusinus (Pinturicchio of Perugia). With perfect mastery, he painted the *trompe-l'oeil* still life on the little shelf, with the silk cloth casting a shadow on the wall and the painting attributes attached to a rosary beneath the cartouche. With this cat and mouse game with visible reality, Pinturicchio consciously placed himself among the legendary painters who could depict anything with miraculous verisimilitude. Pinturicchio presents himself here as no-one less than the Greek painter Zeuxis, about whom it was said that he could paint a bowl of grapes so faithfully that birds actually flew down to eat them.

Originality

Invenzione, the painter's inventivity or originality, was a quality that progressively became more important as fresco painting evolved. Initially, however, pupils had been applauded for emulating their master. This was considered a mark of respect and had the practical advantage of ensuring consistency of style when executing a fresco cycle. It was this that prompted Cennino Cennini to write in his *Artists' Handbook* around 1400: 'Begin by submitting to the guidelines of a master as soon as possible, and do not leave your master before you have to. Always choose the best master with the greatest reputation. Ultimately his spirit and style cannot fail to rub off on you. If you follow a random assortment of masters, you will learn from none of them. That will only lead to inconsistency, for every style will distract your mind.' How very different is Leonardo da Vinci's remark a century later: 'Poor is the pupil who does not surpass his master.' For those who follow others will never surpass them. And those who are unable to create good work themselves are unable to put what they borrow from others to good use.

By this time, imitators were enormously frowned upon in Italy. It was considered a sign of laziness to indiscriminately follow a set of values and dogmas: 'He who thinks little, makes many mistakes.' Originality, the creation of a personal style, a personal signature, had become an absolute precondition for top artistic ranking. A painter was admired as an *alter deus*, as 'another god' who could create something totally new from the material of the visible world. For it is general knowledge that the world has been created not just once, but as many times as there have been original artists.

As in other venerated professions, most of a painter's work is carried out in the mind. *Si pinge con cervello non colla mano* (one paints with the brain, not with the hand). The American neurologist Frank Lynn Meshberger even goes so far as to claim that that is why in the fresco of the *Creation of Adam* on the ceiling of the Sistine Chapel Michelangelo incorporated a cross section of the brain in the contours of the God flying through space. For God gave Adam not only life, but the capacity for creative thought as well.

Originality could manifest itself in many ways. It could be reflected in the rendition of a subject, in the painting technique or in formal aspects, such as the portrayal of the anatomy, facial expression, the rendition of perspective, *trompe l'oeil*, or in any other way the painter set himself apart. At the apex of the Renaissance, around 1500, Leonardo da Vinci and Michelangelo were the first artists to rely on their own genius. Leonardo succeeded in shedding a completely new light on the sacrosanct theme of the *Last Supper* by presenting it as a psychological drama, fraught with emotion, while in the Sistine Chapel Michelangelo ignored the principles of classical art hitherto deemed infallible in creating superhuman figures of dimensions and in postures that defied everything that had ever been taught on proportion. Vasari relates that everyone who was present at the unveiling of the *Last Judgment* in 1541 was astounded at the originality of the fresco (pl. p. 104). The artistic freedom that Michelangelo displayed, Vasari continues, inspired many to defy rule and reason and create something different. Thanks to Michelangelo's example, artists dared to break the chains that previously kept them from experimenting.

At times painters went to extremes to be original. When Giorgione (c. 1477-1510) painted frescoes for the Fondaco de' Tedeschi in Venice, his paintings were so unorthodox – here a woman, there a man, in various postures, one standing beside the head of a lion, another accompanied by an angel in the form of a Cupid – that not even a connoisseur like the artist's biographer Vasari could make head or tail of them, nor could he find 'anybody I questioned who could understand them.' But Giorgione was not looking to be understood: he merely wanted to demonstrate his originality and virtuosity and, above all, wanted to ensure he did not reproduce anyone else's style and work.

64 ORIGINALITY

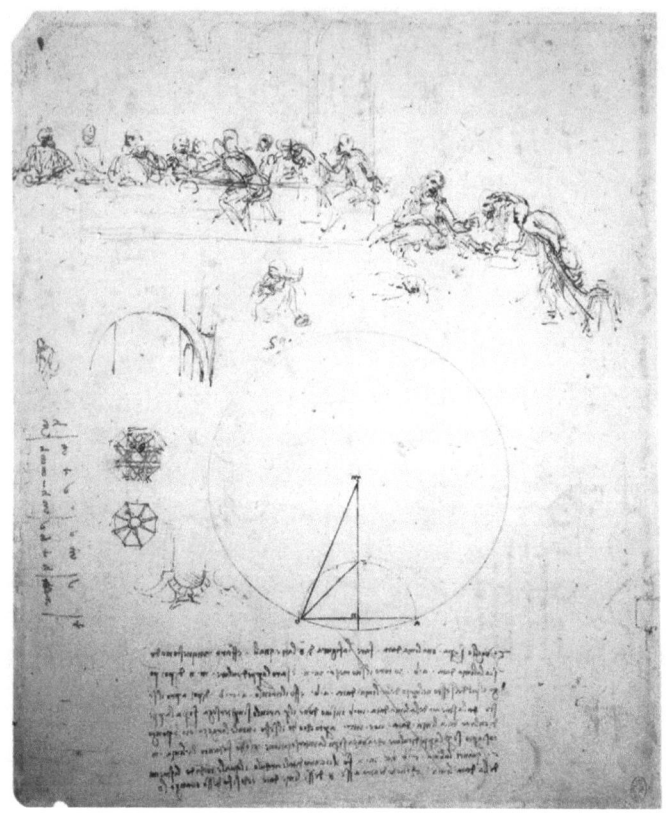

Leonardo da Vinci, Study for the *Last Supper*

Creative Idleness

The tacit obligation to constantly come up with something new had a stimulating effect, but it could also place a heavy mental strain and have a paralysing effect on the painter. Painters were repeatedly seen to suffer from an affliction well known to writers as 'writer's block'. This happened to Pontormo (1494-1557), who during his work often pondered so deeply about what to paint that in the end it stopped him from accomplishing anything at all. And this could go on for weeks or even months.

Leonardo da Vinci suggested ways of overcoming a block and allowing the imagination to wander. 'Look at weathered walls,' he wrote in his *Treatise on Painting (Trattato della pittura,* 'a smouldering wood fire, speckled stones, clouds or mould, for in these irregular shapes you can suddenly see the most unexpected things.' It also helped to go over in your mind's eye what you had seen during the day and to reflect on these observations before going to sleep. Leonardo's contemporary Piero di Cosimo experimented with such mental exercises. He could be totally taken up with looking at a wall or a cloudy sky. In these he would see battles, with horses and the most fantastic cities, and sweeping landscapes that were vaster than you could ever see in reality. Centuries later the Surrealists used the same methods to explore the subconscious of the human mind in order to liberate the imagination from its repressive social strait-jacket. What was later to be dubbed revolutionary, had long been foreshadowed by the Renaissance.

The artist could steer and stimulate the gestation of his ideas by drawing. In the hands of the Renaissance painters drawing became a means of visual thinking. The many studies Leonardo made for the *Battle of Anghiari* and the *Last Supper* (pl. p. 64) clearly demonstrate this. It is as if we can hear him thinking aloud about his own pictorial intentions. Whereas his predecessors repeated the same figures and robes in their studies, as if they were identical siblings, Leonardo's sketches attest to an ongoing creative process in which every form automatically triggered new associations. In his drawings a waterfall could turn into tresses of wavy hair, or a lion's head into the portrait of a warlord. For if the imagination is allowed to flow freely, creative ideas will well up in abundance.

To come up with ideas, an artist had to cultivate a particular mind-set, a certain openness and receptivity. To use an expression of Leonardo da Vinci, he had to make his mind as 'empty as a mirror'. Ideas have to be left to mature, they cannot be forced. Noise and activity will merely drive them away. Hence, the creative process transpires largely out of sight. While a painter might seem to be doing nothing, it is feasible that he is mentally hard at work. Many Renaissance artists practised what may be called 'creative idleness'. For 'great minds (*ingegni elevati*) can accomplish more when they work less, because it is then that they invent new things and come up with those perfect ideas which they go on to express with their hands.' (Vasari).

Needless to say, conservative patrons did not always appreciate such 'creative idleness'. They preferred to see a painter toiling away. A recurring theme in artist's stories is that of the patron hounding the 'misunderstood' artist, taking time off to recharge his imagination. Leonardo da Vinci and the abbot of the monastery of Santa Maria delle Grazie in Milan were always at loggerheads whenever the reverend father caught him 'idling', whether on or off the scaffold. Finally, the matter was referred to the Duke of Milan, Lodovico il Moro, who, of course, sided with Leonardo, for only 'great minds can truly understand art'.

Looking at Frescoes

Narrative Painting

Cycles from the early heydays of fresco painting, the 14th and 15th centuries, generally constituted a coherent whole. The paintings that covered the walls and vaults of churches, chapels, town halls and the interiors of the homes of wealthy merchants and nobles formed a picture story. To enter such interiors is like entering another world, as if you have suddenly stepped into the pages of a picture book. The painted narrative is arranged over two or three registers, one above the other. Starting in the top right-hand corner of the back wall and working clockwise, the chronological story is narrated horizontally all around the interior until it comes back to where it started (pl. p. 42). The next story then commences in the same right-hand corner in the register below. Instead of presenting the stories in chronological order, a painter could also opt for a typological arrangement. This is the case with the *Discovery of the True Cross* in Arezzo in which on facing walls Piero della Francesca (1420–1492) painted paired frescoes depicting similar themes of battles, angels as divine messengers and scenes featuring queens (respectively, the Queen of Sheba and Saint Helena) (pl. pp. 44-45). The arches above the entrance were traditionally reserved for saints and prophets who were only indirectly connected with the narrative depicted on the walls and played no active part in this. The four areas between the cross-ribbed vaults lent themselves by definition to depicting the four evangelists or the four Church Fathers.

Fresco painters devised a number of ways to make it easier for the viewer to follow the storyline. It was primarily the composition that ensured continuity of the storyline. The paintings are like a continuous frieze that automatically leads the viewer's eye from one scene to the next. The action takes place on a sort of narrow podium in the foreground, the background being no more than a summary reference to where the action is located. An abstract representation of rock work with a rudimentary tree is enough to indicate that the scene is set in a landscape, a cluster of finely columned buildings being a *pars pro toto* of a city (pl. p. 41).

Besides denoting location, the background also served to enhance the dramatic effect of a scene. Rock work framing the protagonists draws greater attention to them; the contours of hills guide the viewer's eye to the place of action. The horizons are aligned. The contours of a hill in one scene link up with those in the next; an ascending diagonal line runs on in the scene diagonally above it or continues as a descending line in the next scene in the same register. An even blue sky – an abstract cloudless plane with no indication of the weather or the time of day – canopies the horizon. The protagonists can always be recognised thanks to their unchanging appearance. Even when the narrative spans a long period of time, the figures always appear in the same attire. To depict different emotions, such as anger, amazement, affection or respect, painters utilised a culturally defined set of gestures that the contemporary viewer was familiar with (pl. p.103).

These pictorial formulae served their purpose admirably for many decades. Today, we are still struck by the sense of unity and harmony in a 14th-century chapel with frescoed walls or vault. But the 15th century saw the first signs of change, following the introduction of linear perspective. For this new mathematical system for creating the illusion of depth and distance threatened the visual unity of fresco cycles. In earlier frescoes, the viewer's attention had been focused on the foreground and the flat surface of the wall had been left largely intact. As we have seen, the background was not meant to draw the viewer's attention to details in the background but to support the two-dimensional design of the foreground and throw the protagonists into relief. The purpose of linear perspective, on the other hand, was to draw the eye deeper into the painting. This meant that the viewer had to zoom in on each scene, thereby breaking the continuous rhythm (pl. p. 42-43). Linear perspective led to fragmentation of the fresco cycle, disrupting the flow and harmony of the overall work. The continuous sequence of scenes that typified traditional fresco painting was irretrievably lost. But it was replaced by something new. With the advent of linear perspective, a new pictorial formula came into vogue that was to remain popular until well into the 18th century. This new formula transformed fresco painting into a sophisticated form of ambient art. From then on, the imaginary space of the fresco veraciously replicated real space, and the fresco painter had attained his goal if he succeeded in dishing up deception as truth.

Ambient Art

By the last quarter of the 15th century, the pictorial formula of rows of scenes one above the other had come to be regarded as somewhat dated, but this did not mean it was written off entirely. Old-style frescoes continued to be painted, even as major projects, such as the murals in the choir of the Santa Maria Novella, one of the main churches of Florence. Here, at the close of the 15th century, Domenico Ghirlandaio painted a huge cycle of frescoes for the Tornabuoni family, as if the old formula had lost none of its lustre. He compiled his scenes in the usual manner, row by row. At the same time, Ghirlandaio showed himself to be a man of the time. His paintings integrated the latest innovations, with full mastery of linear perspective, a perfect rendition of anatomy and physiognomy, and, as was fashionable at the time, settings that combined elements of contemporary architecture with those borrowed from classical antiquity. But the way in which he chose to arrange the frescoes was no different from that of Giotto's 200-year-old narrative scheme.

Meanwhile, twenty years had passed since Andrea Mantegna (c. 1430-1506) had applied an entirely novel concept in his frescoes in the *Camera degli Sposi* in the

Palazzo Ducale in Mantua. Mantegna's approach differed in two important respects from that of Ghirlandaio in the Santa Maria Novella. Mantegna limited himself to one main scene on each wall, thereby adopting the principle of classical theatre, namely, that of unity of time, place and action. Moreover, Mantegna used his knowledge of linear perspective to depict the scene as if it were actually happening before our eyes. The boundary between actual space and illusory space in the painting has vanished. It has been conjured away to make space for an imaginary world of the painter which the viewer feels he can step into any time he wishes. At one end of the room there is a hilly landscape, on the other wall we see the life-size figures of patron Ludovico Gonzaga surrounded by his family and courtiers on a slightly raised podium (pl. p. 46 above). To make it more plausible how they got up there, Mantegna has even thought of painting a flight of steps alongside the mantelpiece. An assortment of details reinforces the impression that we – the viewers and the persons portrayed – are all in the same room. A curtain hangs from a feigned rod as though it separates the space we seemingly share with the marquis from another which it appears to screen off; a courtier standing in front of a painted column with a deceptively real capital, seems to be in our space; a painted curtain has been drawn aside from the doorway, and so on. Not only did Mantegna use his revolutionary approach for the walls, he applied the principle of extending natural space to the ceilings, too. Through a round hole we catch a glimpse of the pale blue sky and a few clouds floating past (pl. p. 98 below). We see laughing faces overlooking the parapet. A flower tub balances precariously on a rod above our heads, and *putti*, literally viewed from below, have clambered over the parapet and are now poised above our heads. Never before had a painter so convincingly created a surrogate reality.

The *Camera degli Sposi* marked the start of a new development in interior decoration which was to be long lived. For three centuries it would lose nothing of its vitality. Time and again, painters devised new optical tricks to blur the boundary between reality and illusion. They did away with wainscotting to create paintings from floor level, and added false doors to the architecture through which someone appears to enter (Paolo Veronese, Villa Barbaro, Maser, pl. p. 46 below); they extended floor tiles and columns into the wall (Baldassare Peruzzi, Villa Farnesina, Rome) or painted the Forge of Vulcan on either side of the fireplace (Giulio Romano, Palazzo del Te, Mantua). In Baroque churches they sought to extend reality towards heaven, replacing stone vaults with a vision of angels and saints aswirl in a radiant and golden sky. Such visionary scenes were meant to allow the believer a foretaste of the heavenly paradise that awaited them if they followed the path set out for them by the church (pl. p. 99, 100). All the visual interventions which painters invented over the years served one and the same purpose, namely, to satisfy man's deep-seated need for escape into illusion.

Painters were compelled to stretch their artistic powers to the extreme to come up with ever-stronger visual effects. Mantegna makes us feel spatially close to the figures he depicted in his *Camera degli Sposi*, but they seem unaware of our presence or at least they make no apparent attempt to make contact with us. This is different in his later frescoes. In these there is a dynamic interaction between the painting and the public, whereby the viewer is constantly tossed back and forth by *trompe l'oeil* and foreshortening. One moment we are sucked into infinite space, the next we are thrust back by an equally powerful counter-movement, with figures with outstretched arms and feet emerging from the picture plane or hurtling towards us at an alarming speed (pl. p. 47).

Compared with the 14th century, frescoes now had a far greater immediacy and expressivity. But this came at the expense of narrative diversity. In the Scrovegni Chapel, Giotto still had the luxury of being able to spread the life stories of Christ and the Virgin over 40 frescoes. But the requirement of spatial uniformity which later frescoes were obliged to meet reduced the number of scenes that could be depicted. Painters managed to circumvent this limitation to some extent by incorporating what may be called frame narratives: paintings in which other scenes are also embedded. The painters allocated different types of themes to different locations and ostensibly different media. Secondary scenes were depicted on quasi-bronze plaques and allegoric scenes were painted in *grisaille* (marble stucco) to distinguish them from the images of real people of flesh and blood. Lastly, the most important scenes could be isolated from the rest by presenting them in framed paintings (*quadri riportati*), which were given pride of place in the architectural setting (Annibale Caracci, Palazzo Farnese, Rome, pl. p. 48). Painted, feigned architecture (*quadratura*) as an overarching structure was also used to help bring together multiple scenes (pl. p. 100). With these devices, painters were still able to accommodate a reasonable number of scenes without jeopardising the continuity of the narrative.

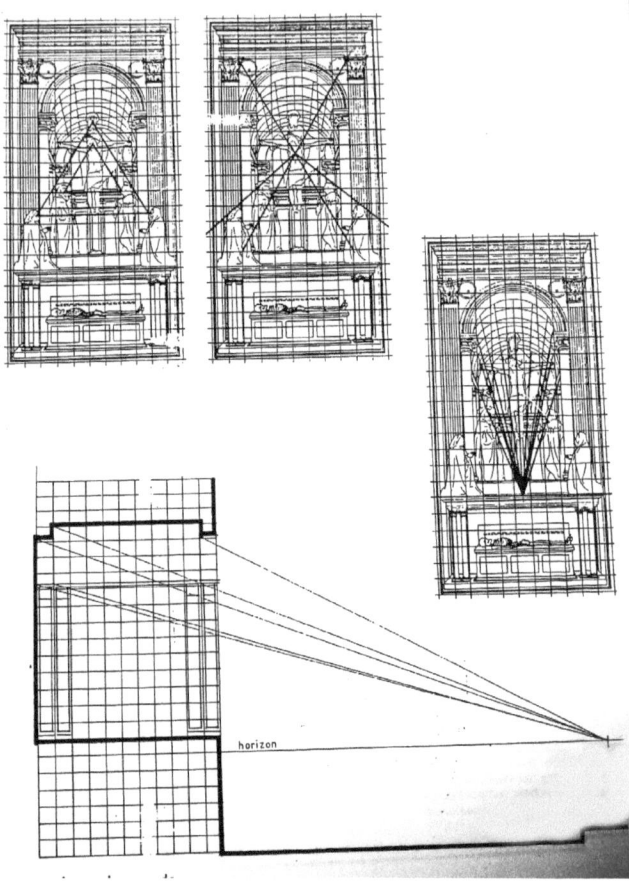
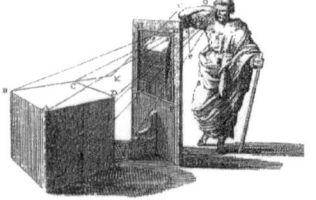

Linear Perspective

The discovery of linear perspective provided a whole new premise for fresco cycles. Filippo Brunelleschi (mainly famous for engineering the dome of the Florence Cathedral) was probably the first to systematically examine the effect of linear perspective. He did so around 1415 when he painted a number of Florentine buildings so that they exactly replicated the actual buildings from a given viewpoint. He checked the likeness by drilling a hole in the panel, turning the panel round and looking through the hole at the image reflected in a mirror he held at arm's length. When he lowered the mirror, he was left with a view of the actual building identical to the mirror image of the painted panel. Brunelleschi's experiments with the mirror led to the development of linear perspective. The basic principle of this is that lines perpendicular to the picture plane – which in reality run parallel to each other – seem to converge at a common vanishing point, in much the same way as the railway lines seem to come together at an imaginary point in the distance. The main drawback to linear perspective was its static character. A perspectival construction is only truly convincing when the viewer-looks at the painting with one eye, like an archer, from a point on the axial line.

The Renaissance found support for systematisation of linear perspective in classic treatises on optics, especially by Euclid (c. 300 BC). He claimed that: 'If sections of equal length of a line are placed in a straight line, those farthest away appear to be smaller (...); the distances between parallel lines look unequal when viewed from a distance; the distance between equidistant lines that lie below eye level appears to be smaller from a distance.' The Arabian mathematician Alhazen (965–c. 1040) corrected and elaborated Euclid's theories in his *Book of Optics* (1021). Alhazen's book was translated into Latin around 1200 and an Italian version became available at the end of the 14th century. Renaissance artists made grateful use of this to substantiate the theory of linear perspective.

Leon Battista Alberti committed the principles of linear perspective to writing. The importance he attached to linear perspective is apparent from the disproportionately long section he devoted to this in his *Treatise on Painting* (*De Pictura*), which he dedicated to Brunelleschi in 1435. Alberti construed perception as bundles of rays that connected the eye with the perceived object. They were subject to the laws of geometry. A longitudinal section of this bundle shows a triangle, the top of which corresponds with the observer's eye, the base with the perceived object. The more distant the object, the more elongated the triangle and the narrower its base. Comparing a painting to a window Alberti realised that the objects on it can be made to obey the same laws of geometry as the visual rays.

Alberti offered the following guidelines for constructing a perspectival framework:

- Parallel lines perpendicular to the picture plane (the orthogonal lines) should converge at a common vanishing point.
- The distance between equidistant lines parallel to the picture plane (the transversal lines) should appear to become progressively smaller as they recede into the distance.
- The floor tile pattern that the orthogonal and transversal lines creates enables the painter to scale objects and figures in the background.

Many painters faithfully followed Alberti's guidelines. Fifteenth-century paintings are rife with the tiled floors that aided the construction of the perspective. As painters grew more accustomed to working with perspective, they no longer had a need for such aids. From that moment, tiled floors are no longer omnipresent. Especially in the field of fresco painting the introduc-

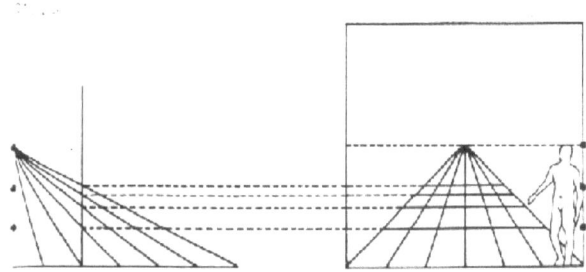

tion of linear perspective had a tremendous impact. It opened the exciting possibility to bring the far away world of heroes and saints much nearer. As we have seen in the last chapter, as a result of the application of linear perspective the boundaries between the real and the illusory space became blurred and it took, metaphorically speaking, a small step to enter the painted world. The archetypal example of linear perspective is the large fresco of the *Holy Trinity* (pl. p. 80, 97) in the Santa Maria Novella in Florence, which Masaccio painted in 1425, probably in close communication or even cooperation with Brunelleschi. The fresco features three spatial zones: a painted sarcophagus set back beneath an altar table that appears to protrude from the picture plane; the two patrons parallel to the picture plane; and finally a magnificent, deeply recessed Renaissance vaulted chapel with the *Holy Trinity*. Since the vanishing point of the orthogonal lines is at eye level, the viewer looks up at the vaulted hall from below. The ceiling cassettes perform the role of the tiled floor and provide a perspectival framework like that which Alberti described. The way the vaulted hall systematically recedes into the background made it possible for the first time to reconstruct a floor plan from a painted building and to determine its dimensions. This was very different from the work of previous generations of painters, who placed people in box-like buildings barely large enough for them to sit down in.

Linear perspective also proved an extremely valuable aid for painting frescoes in cupolas or vaults. This form of perspective, *di sotto in su* (as it was called in contemporary literature), literally 'from the bottom up', was first developed in Northern Italy (Mantegna, *Camera degli Sposi,* Mantua (pl. p. 98 below); Correggio, painting of the cupola of the San Giovanni Evangelista and the Duomo of Parma (pl. p. 99)). *Di sotto in su* figures move along the viewer's line of sight and are therefore depicted with strong foreshortening. The many frescoes in cupolas and vaults of baroque churches in Rome are painted almost without exception *di sotto in su*. The extension of the actual architecture with feigned architecture (*quadratura*) leads the eye upwards. From there the eye soars even higher up into the heavens, transported in a vortex of saints and angels to a vanishing point invariably marked by a symbol or being of supra-mundane order. There, the blurring of contours and blending of colours into a golden heavenly fulgor strengthens the illusion of infinite space. A specialist in painting *quadratura* was the Jesuit Andrea Pozzo (1642-1709), the painter of the impressive vault paintings in the Sant'Ignazio in Rome (pl. p. 100). The Sant'Ignazio is one of the few baroque churches without a cupola. But Pozzo's mastery of *quadratura* and *di sotto in su* enabled him to give the church a fake cupola, which, from a certain viewpoint, can hardly be distinguished from the real thing. In his two-volume manual on architectural perspectival drawing, *Perspectiva pictorum et architectorum* (1698), Pozzo explains his working methods. First he made detailed sketches based on the height and dimensions of the vault and calculations of the curvature of the vault. An enlarged version of these sketches was then copied onto a grid of squares. Next he spanned a network of cords across the ceiling of the nave, which enabled him to project the squared grid onto the ceiling. Pozzo's book became the standard reference work for fresco painters of late baroque churches throughout Europe. It enjoyed many reprints and was translated into French, German, English and, ultimately, even Chinese.

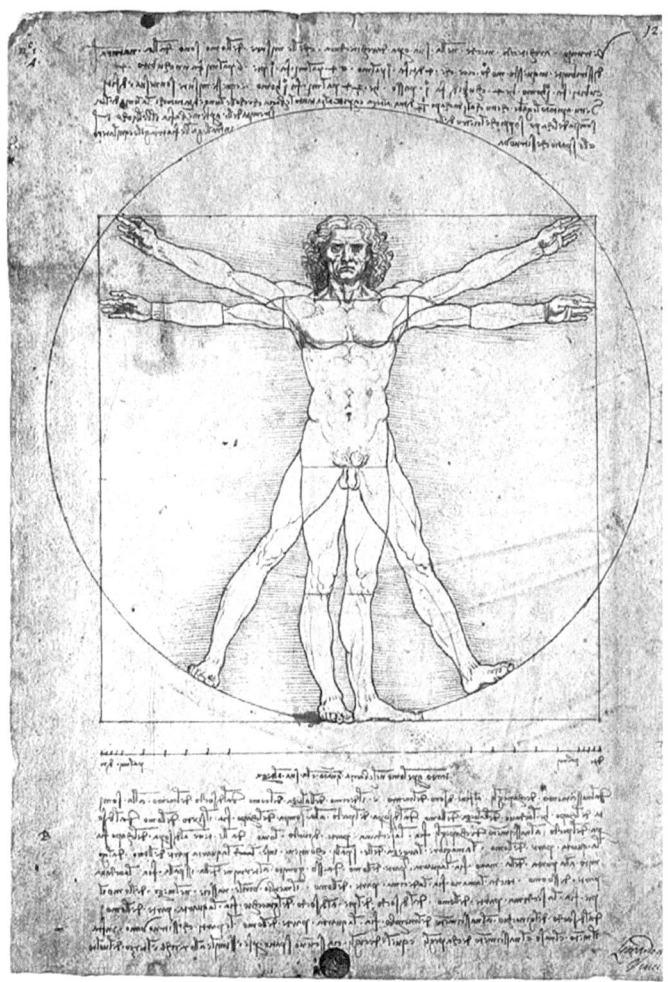

Leonardo da Vinci, *Vitruvius Man*

Naked Beauty

The depiction of the human body was one of the cornerstones of Italian fresco painting. While landscapes, animals and other subjects were appreciated in northern countries, in Italian art motifs that had no direct connection with humankind were accorded a minor role or were entirely absent. In his fresco of the days of creation in the Sistine Chapel, Michelangelo went so far as to omit the days of the creation of fish and animals and confined himself exclusively to man (depicting God as a human being). The Italian Renaissance had a high opinion of man and his calling. The old Christian idea of man as a sinner was rivalled by another Christian idea, that of man's creation in the image and likeness of God. Pico della Mirandola, in his *Oration on the Dignity of Man* (*Oratio de hominis dignitate*, 1487) has God address Adam with the following words: 'I have placed you at the world's centre so that you may thence more easily look around at whatever is in the world. I have made you neither of heaven nor of earth, neither mortal nor immortal, so that you may, as the free and extraordinary shaper of yourself, fashion yourself into whatever form you choose.' It was the artist's task to help man grasp his exalted task of perfecting himself like a good painter or able sculptor. Here he emulated classical sculpture, which commanded so much interest in the Renaissance. For Greek and Roman sculptors strove to present man in a divine form. In their pursuit of an absolute and unchanging beauty ideal, they established a canon of the human body, a harmonious system of the relative proportions of all body parts, in relation to each other as well as to the body as a whole. For the Renaissance artist, the works of Vitruvius, the Roman architect and theoretician, formed the touchstone here. Based on systematic measurement of the human body, Vitruvius had produced a detailed guide to its proportions. The ingenious machinery of the human body, however, was greater than the sum of its parts. Vitruvius showed that the human body also fitted into the perfect geometrical shapes of the circle and the square. A man standing erect with his arms spread fits into a square (*homo ad quadratum*); a man with his legs apart at a certain angle and his outstretched arms raised to the level of his crown fits into a circle (*homo ad circulum*, pl. p. 86.). Renaissance artists, including Leonardo da Vinci, were most intrigued by this so-called Vitruvian Man, and they often depicted him. Similarly, many figures in frescoes were inspired by the Vitruvian Man.

Human beauty could only be fully appreciated when figures were naked; the ancients preferred to project their beauty ideals on nude males in their prime. In classical antiquity naked beauty symbolised spiritual beauty. This notion made a triumphant comeback in the Renaissance. Italian artists seized every opportunity to incorporate nudes or semi-nudes in their paintings. Of course, not all subjects lent themselves to this. But the story of Adam and Eve, the crucifixion of Christ, and tales of certain saints

(Saint Sebastian) were a good excuse to show the human body in all its glory. Above all, commissions for paintings of the Last Judgement provided unique opportunities for painters to show what they were capable of in this respect. The gigantic frescoes of Luca Signorelli of the *Resurrection*, *Hell* and *Heavenly Paradise* in the San Brizio Chapel of the Duomo of Orvieto (1499-1504) are a veritable exposition of human nudity (pl. p. 101 below). Forty years later, Michelangelo went one step further in his *Last Judgment* fresco in the Sistine Chapel. In this, hundreds of nudes make up a complete pictorial encyclopaedia of the human body. Some painters could not resist depicting nudes and included them in scenes that were inappropriate. What is the reason for portraying the beggar as a classic, athletic nude in the fresco of the *Appearance of Maria in the Temple* (Ghirlandaio, choir of the Santa Maria Novella, pl. p. 101 above)? And why are the two beautiful sons of Noah on the vault of the Sistine Chapel so shocked by the nakedness of their drunken father while, contrary to the logic of the story, they themselves are depicted without clothes?

As time went by, the church became more critical of the unbridled portrayal of nudes, at least in religious contexts. The first sounds of protest could be heard at the onset of the 16th century. Appealing as it was to senses, a nude Saint Sebastian painted by Fra Bartolommeo was removed from a church after monks taking confession had discovered that some women had sinned after admiring this ravishing and vividly realistic representation of the saint. Fra Bartolommeo himself likewise repented his ways, and piously brought paintings and drawings of nudes to the pyre of vanities that the preacher of penitence, Savonarola, had erected on a square in Florence in 1497. In the 16th century, the protests grew louder and more frequent. The Dutch Pope Adrian VI (1522-1523) proposed removing the Sistine frescoes. The Counter-Reformation brought increasing support for his plan. In the end, a compromise was agreed. The frescoes could stay, but a former pupil of Michelangelo, Daniele da Volterra, nicknamed Il Braghettone (the 'Breeches Maker'), was commissioned to cover the vital parts of the many hundreds of Michelangelo's nudes with painted loincloths or fig leaves. A similar fate awaited all the other frescoes in Italian churches. The only frescoes to be spared were those in secular settings, such as palaces and villas. Recent restorations have usually removed these additions. During the restoration of the fresco of the Last Judgment in the Sistine Chapel, however, it was decided to preserve some of the concealing garments as an historical given.

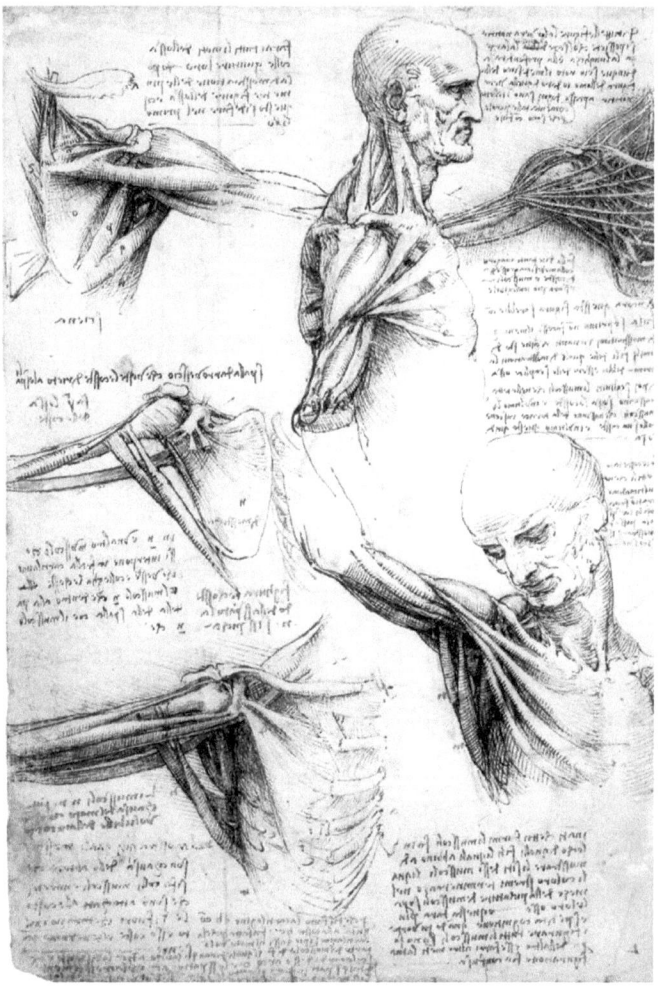

Leonardo da Vinci, Anatomical studies

Anatomist-Artist

Artists had a number of ways of practising depicting the human body. The studios were crammed with plaster casts of body parts and classical statues. They also painted from life models. Assistants and pupils took it in turns to pose for each other in postures that were later elaborated in the frescoes. Models posed nude throughout the year but for their well-being this was largely concentrated in the summer months. To help the models maintain a difficult pose, they were provided with studio props, such as foot rests, pillars to lean against, or a rope to hold on to. Posing nude occurred more often than strictly necessary since it had become common practice to work from nude models for figures that were clothed in the final fresco. Alberti had prescribed that figures should be constructed from the inside. He meant this quite literally. An artist had to start with the skeletal structure, and then add the pertinent muscles and sinews, and cover these with fat and skin. Finally he had to dress the figure with drapery. Only in this manner would a painter manage to construct a credible representation of the human figure. A study of a soldier in the foreground of Mantegna's fresco of *Saint James Led to His Execution* reveals that the artist had followed

Alberti's advice. The soldier in the study was drawn nude; in the completed fresco in the Ovetari Chapel in Padua he adopts the same posture, but is now decorously dressed in a soldier's *tunica*. Studies of male nudes were more frequent than those of women, and if necessary, studies of males could be 'transgendered' into women in the final fresco, as shown by the male study that was used for the Libyan Sibyl in the Sistine Chapel (pl. p. 102). Other artists used female models or their mistresses, while some painters made their artistic observations of nudes at the baths.

The real revolution in figure painting did not dawn until artists started dissecting corpses or watching others do so. This became common practice from the last quarter of the 15th century, after Pope Sixtus IV (1471-1484) had given permission for corpses to be dissected in certain instances. The corpses of executed persons with no hope of salvation in the afterlife and those of unidentified foreigners could be used for this purpose. Human dissection primarily served medical science, but it also allowed artists to gain a first-hand insight into the inner make-up of the human body. It opened their eyes to a whole new world. Here was an area in which Renaissance artists had a chance to outstrip their much admired predecessors from classical antiquity. Classical art was not based on knowledge of the inner structure of the human body. Even the uncontested authority on medical matters, the famous physician Galen from Pergamum (2nd century AD), had only a limited insight; for his knowledge was primarily based on the dissection of monkeys and pigs, since there was a taboo against the dissection of human beings. Antonio del Pollaiuolo (ca. 1431-98) was one of the first, if not the very first, artist to have personally examined the internal structure of the body. He very likely owed his experience to his cooperation with the Florentine physician Antonio Benivieni, a friend of Lorenzo de' Medici and a pioneer in the field of autopsy. Pollauiolo applied his new anatomical knowledge to his engraving of *The Battle of Ten Naked Men* (fig. p. 96), which had a great impact on later painting, as can be seen in Signorelli's frescoes in the San Brizio Chapel in Orvieto (pl. p. 101 below).

Artists with influential patrons were also given the opportunity to dissect corpses. Leonardo da Vinci dissected some thirty corpses during his lifetime, hundreds of studies of which have been preserved (pl. p. 92). Michelangelo was a devoted anatomist, too. The prior of the monastery of Santo Spirito, Niccolò Bichiellini, provided him with a room in the monastery hospital where he could carry out his post mortem research undisturbed. The biographer Condivi tells that Michelangelo persisted with this vile, disturbing work until he was on the point of becoming seriously ill from the prolonged contact with dead bodies, and had to rest. But anatomic material was hard to come by and most artists had to acquire their knowledge as best they could. Driven by curiosity, some artists – Signorelli and Rosso Fiorentino – allegedly had no qualms about clandestinely digging up corpses in graveyards for purposes of their own studies. So great was their curiosity about the secrets of the functioning of the human body.

This scrupulous observation of the human body was sometimes at odds with the idealizing precepts of classical antiquity. Not every figure can be squeezed into a straitjacket of predetermined proportions. The one is tall or fat, the other short or thin. Even Leonardo, who had so successfully illustrated Vitruvius's ideal human prototype, criticised artists who had no eye for the infinite number of variations that were possible in nature and who applied the same formula to all the figures they painted as if they were multiple twins.

Artists endeavoured to resolve the dilemma by opting for a compromise between their observation of anatomical reality and the heroism of classical art. This resulted in a form of 'selective realism' by which figures were constructed from a selection of carefully observed body parts. For the fresco painter constantly sought to combine the artist and scientist in himself.

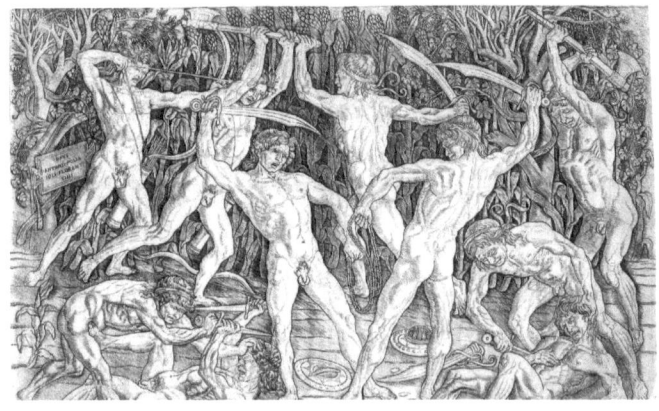

Antonio del Pollaiuolo, *Battle of the Ten Nudes*, 1465, *engraving*

Next page: Masaccio, *Holy Trinity*, c. 1425, Santa Maria Novella, Florence

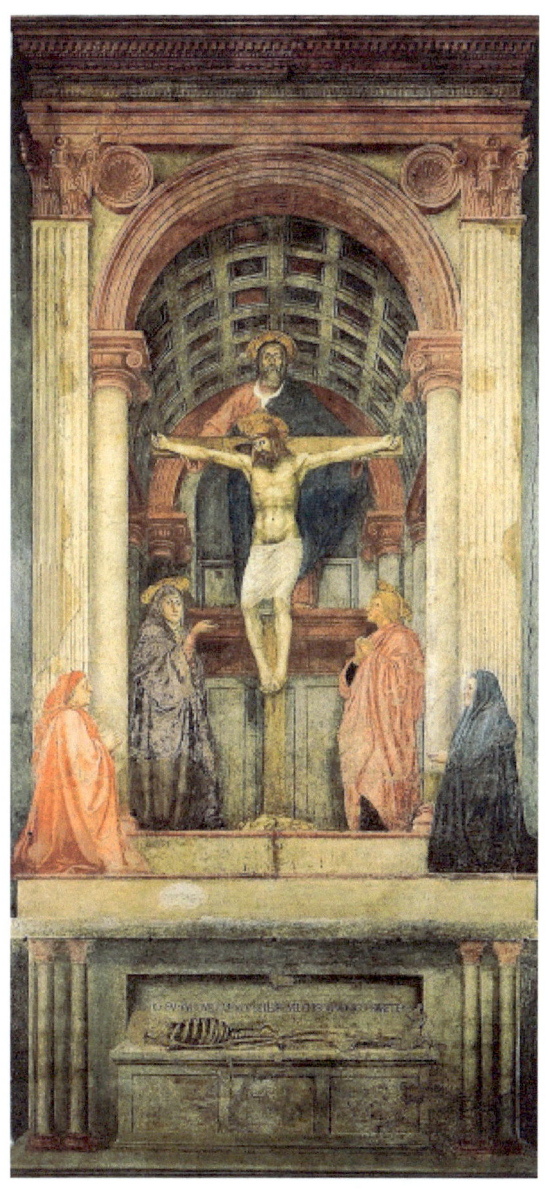

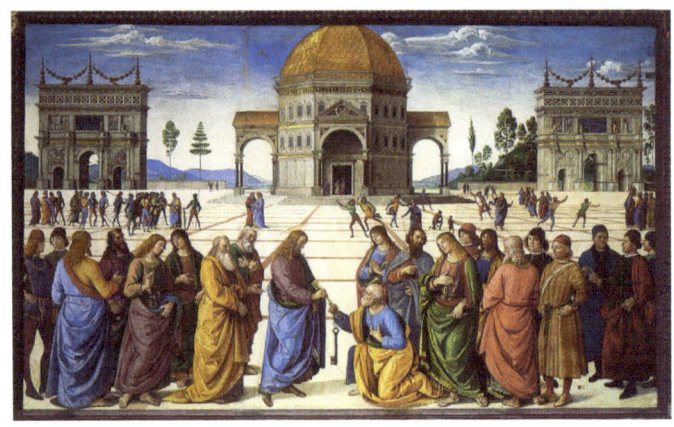

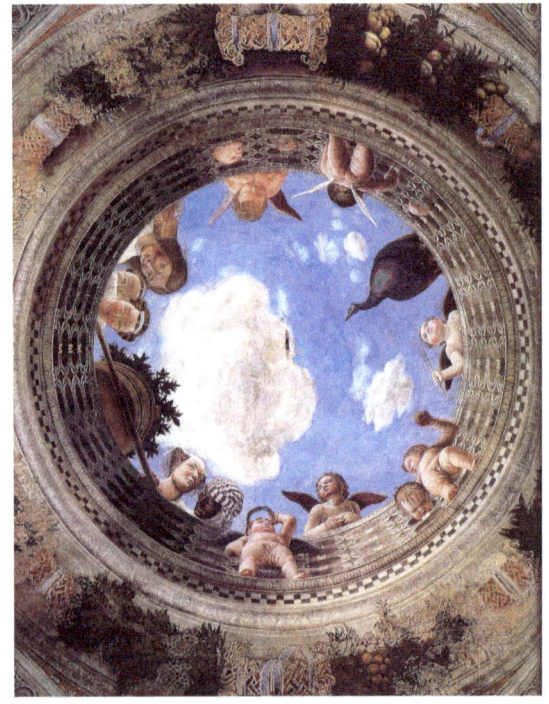

LINEAR PERSPECTIVE 99

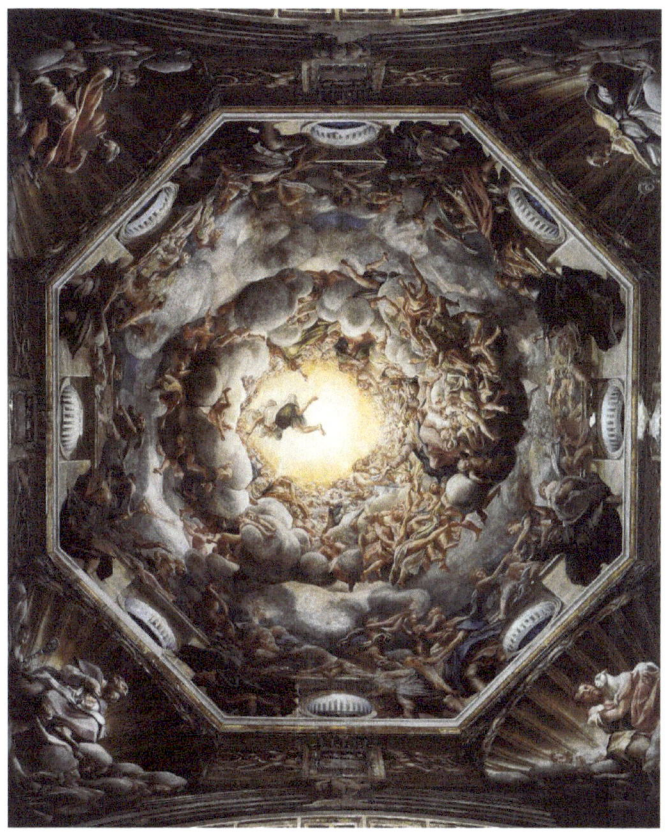

Next page: above Perugino, *Giving of the Keys to St. Peter,* 1481, Sistine Chapel, Vatican

Below: Mantegna, di sotto in su perspective, *Camera degli Sposi*, Palazzo Ducale, Mantua

Above: Correggio, *Assumption*, 1526-1530, Cupola Duomo Parma

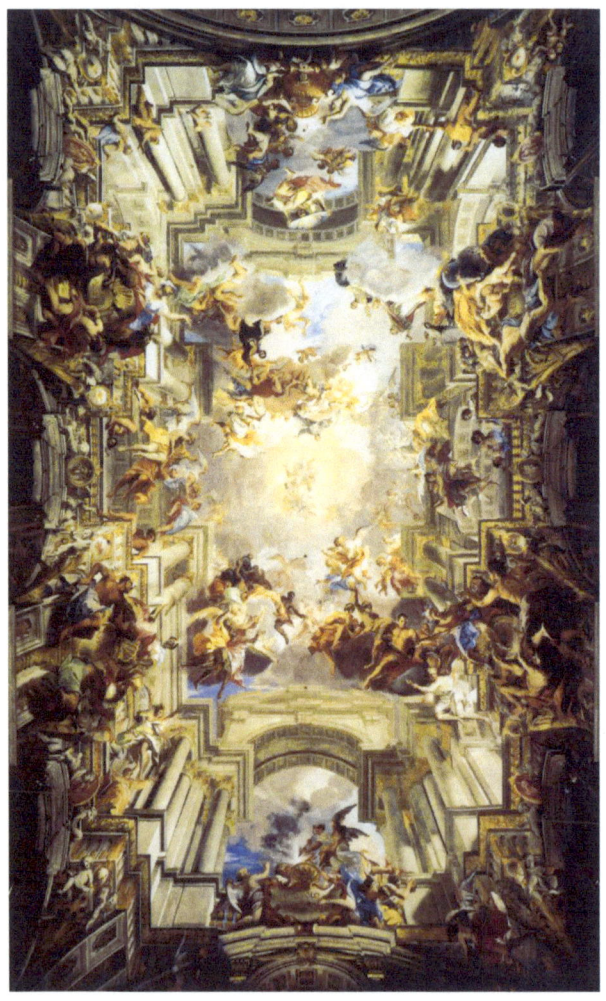

Andrea Pozzo, *Allegory of the Missionary Work of the Jesuits,* 1691-1694, S. Ignazio, Rome

Next page: Above: D. Ghirlandaio, *Presentation of the Virgin* (detail), 1486-1490, Santa Maria Novella, Florence
Below: Luca Signorelli, *The Blessed* (detail), 1499-1503, San Brizio Chapel, Duomo Orvieto

NAKED BEAUTY

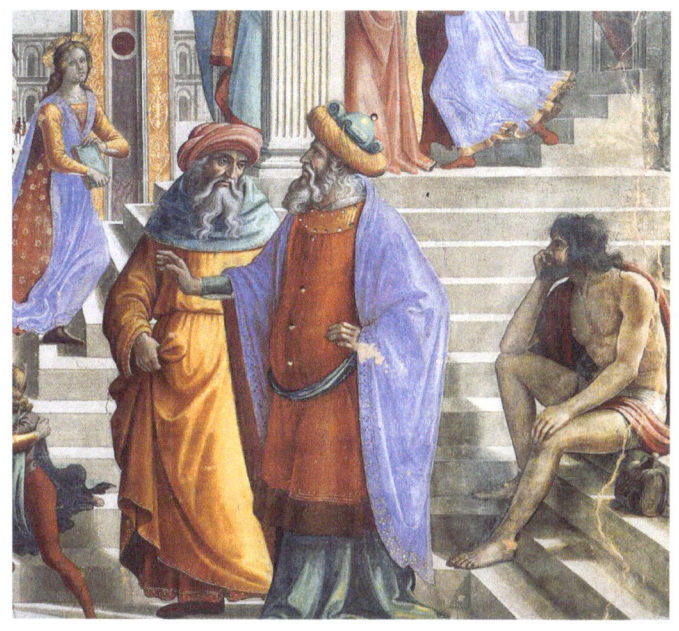

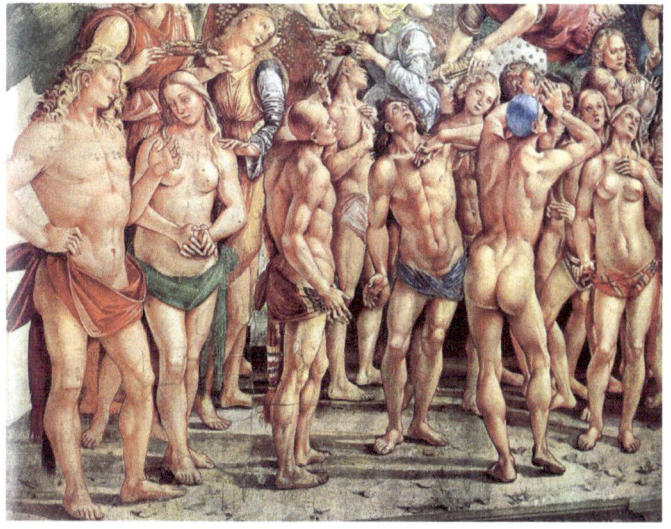

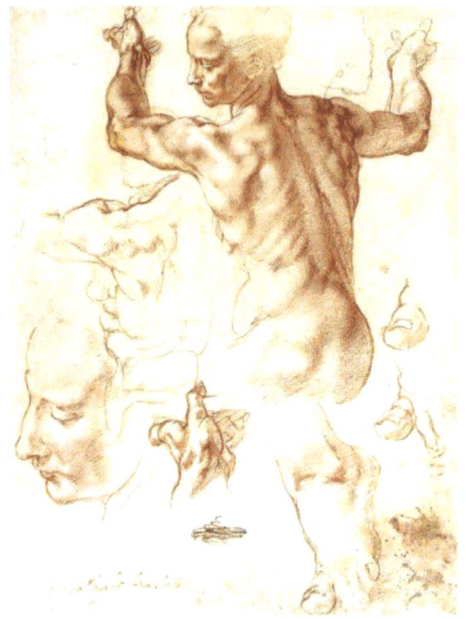
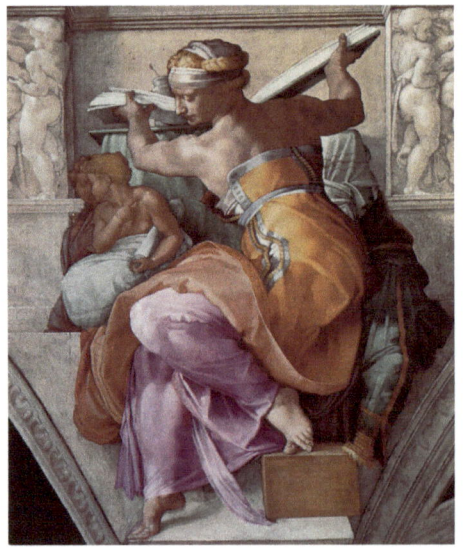

BODY AND SOUL

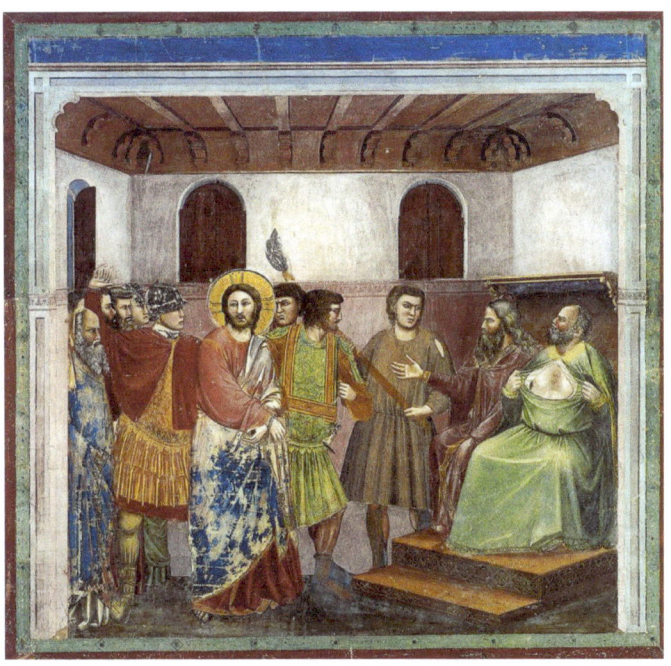

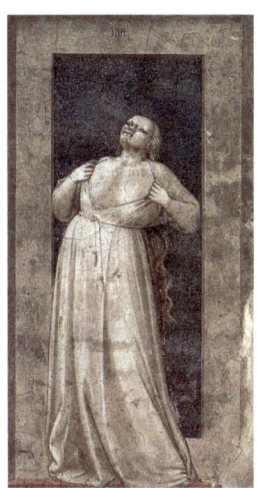

Next page: Study and fresco of the *Libyan Sibyl*, ceiling Sistine Chapel, Vatican

Above Giotto, *Christ before Caiaphas*, and right, *Wrath* (Ira) c. 1305, Scrovegni Chapel, Padua

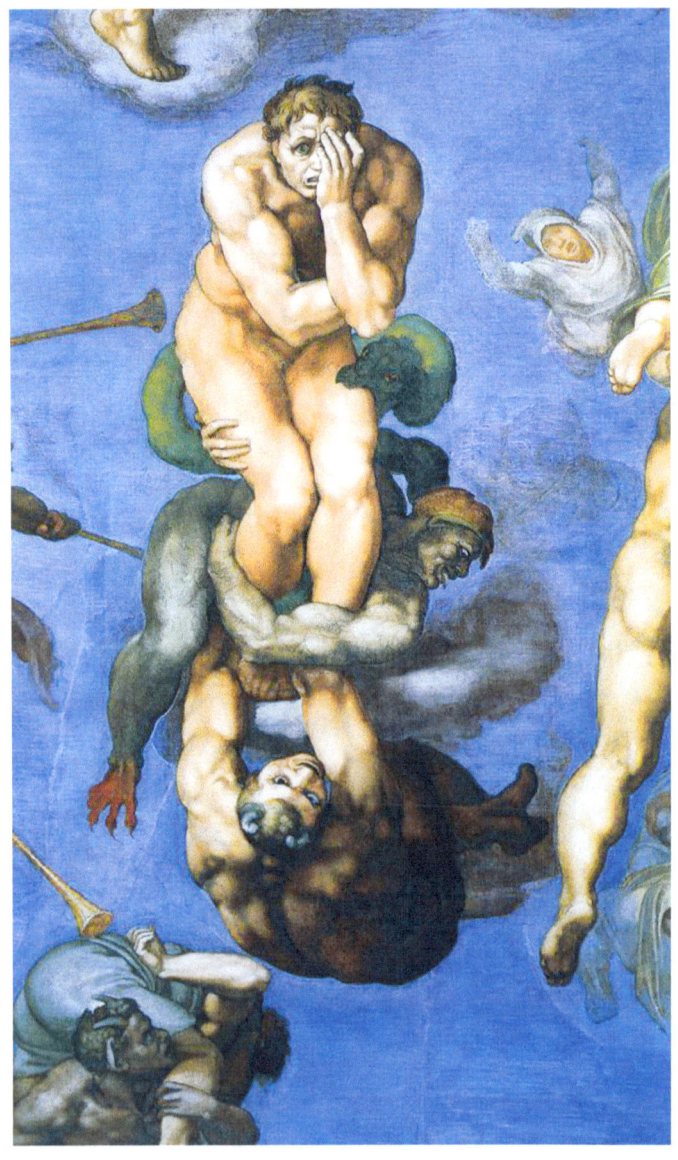

CHRONOLOGICAL OVERVIEW 105

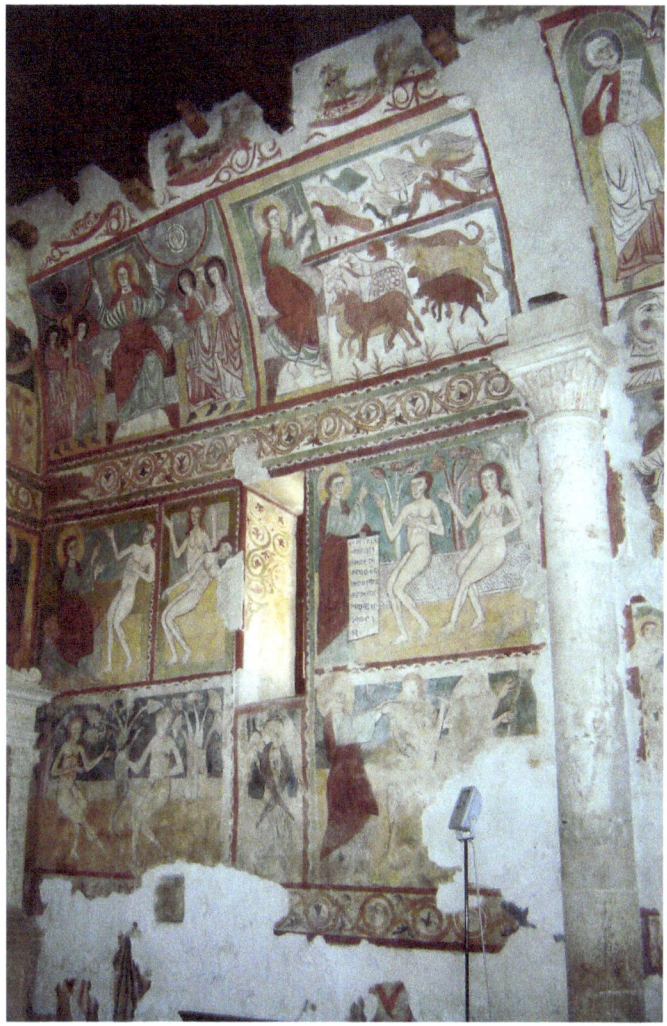

Next page: Michelangelo, *Last Judgment* (detail), 1534-1541, Sistine Chapel, Vatican

Above: Frescoes of the *Genesis*, 13C, Santa Maria ad Cryptas, Fossa

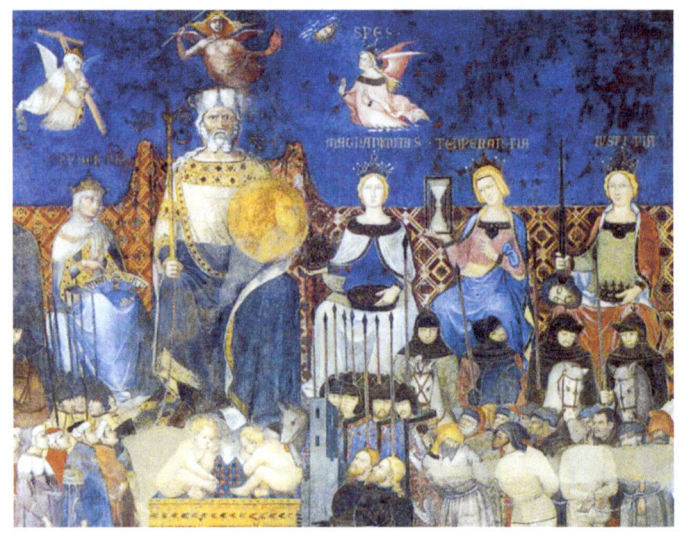

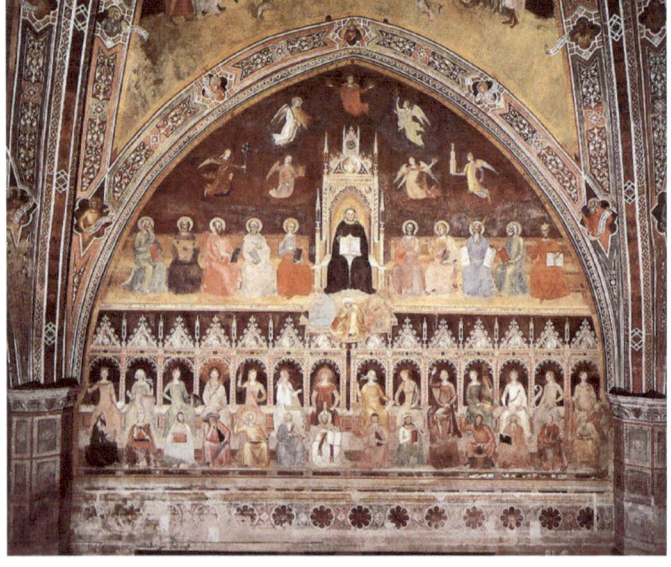

CHRONOLOGICAL OVERVIEW 107

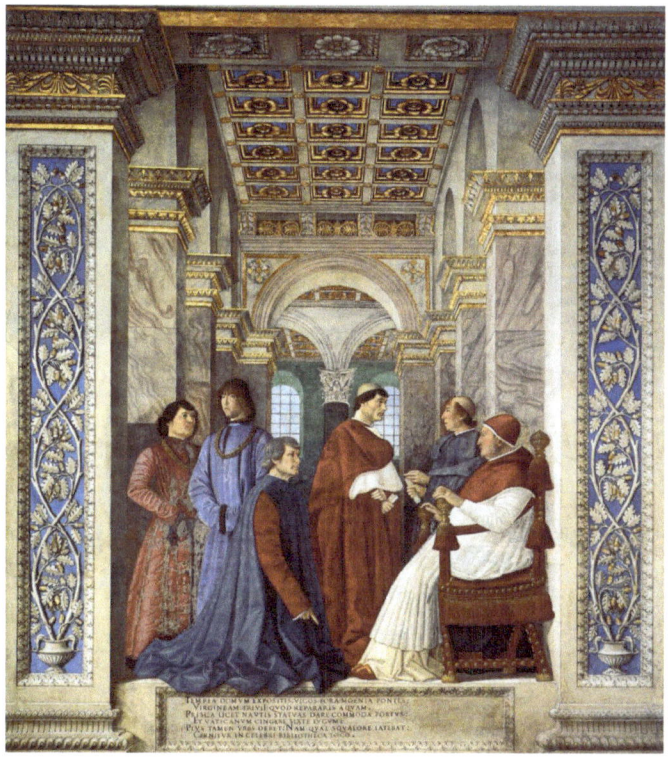

Next page: above, Ambrogio Lorenzetti, *Allegory of Good Goverment* (detail), 1338-1340, Palazzo Pubblico, Siena
Below: Andrea da Firenze, *Apotheosis of St. Thomas Aquinas*, 1365-1368, Spanish Chapel, Santa Maria Novella, Florence

Above: Melozzo da Forli, *Sixtus IV Appointing Platina*, 1474-1477, Pinacoteca Vatican

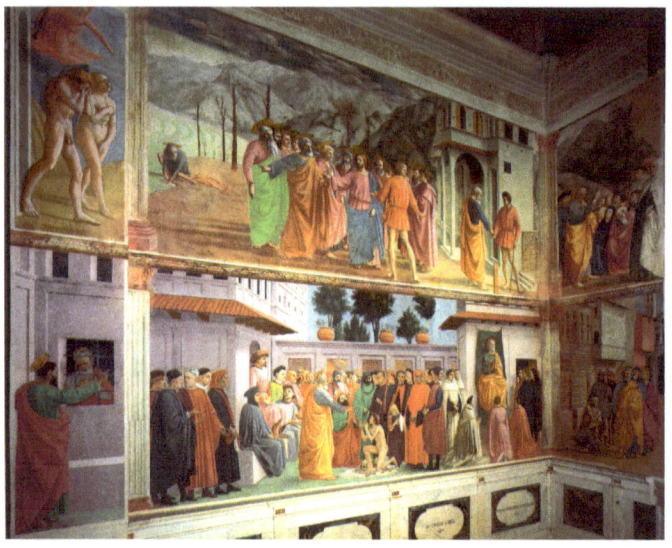

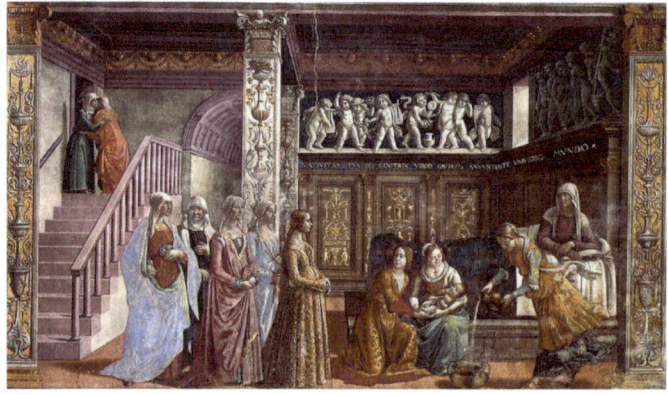

Above: Masaccio and Masolino (1424-1427) Filippino Lippi (1481-1482), Brancacci Chapel, Santa Maria del Carmine, Florence

Below: Ghirlandaio, *Birth of the Virgin*, 1486-1491, Santa Maria Novella, Florence

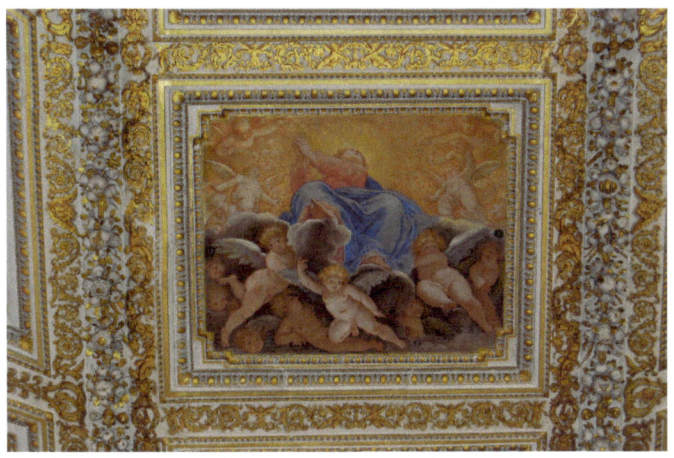

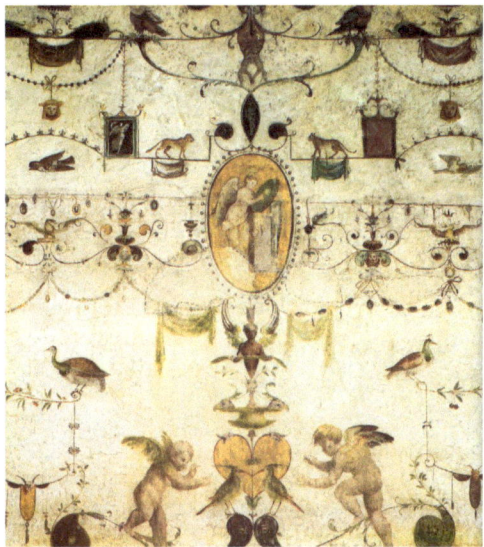

Above: Il Pomarancio, ceiling frescoes New Sacristy, 1605-1615, Santa Maria di Loreto
Below: Giovanni da Udine, grotesques, Loggia di Bibbiena, 1516, Vatican

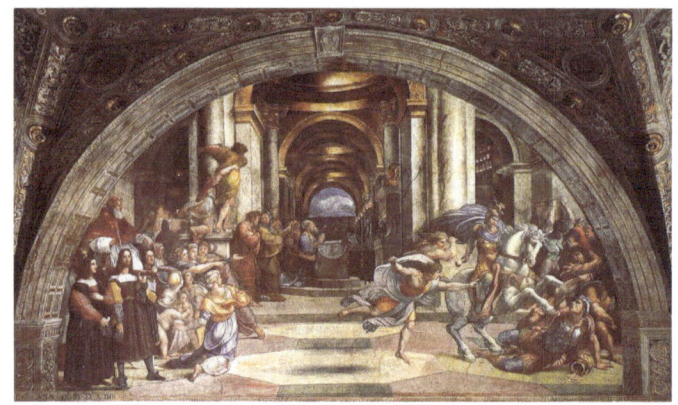
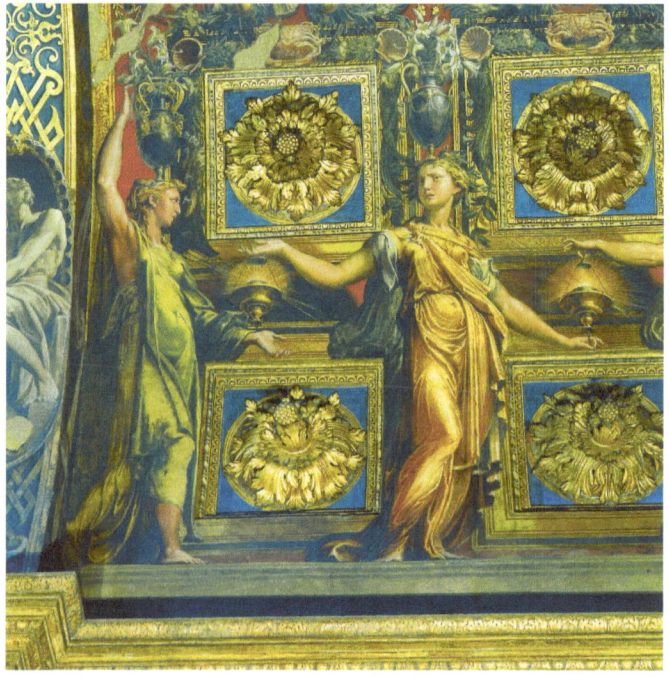

CHRONOLOGICAL OVERVIEW

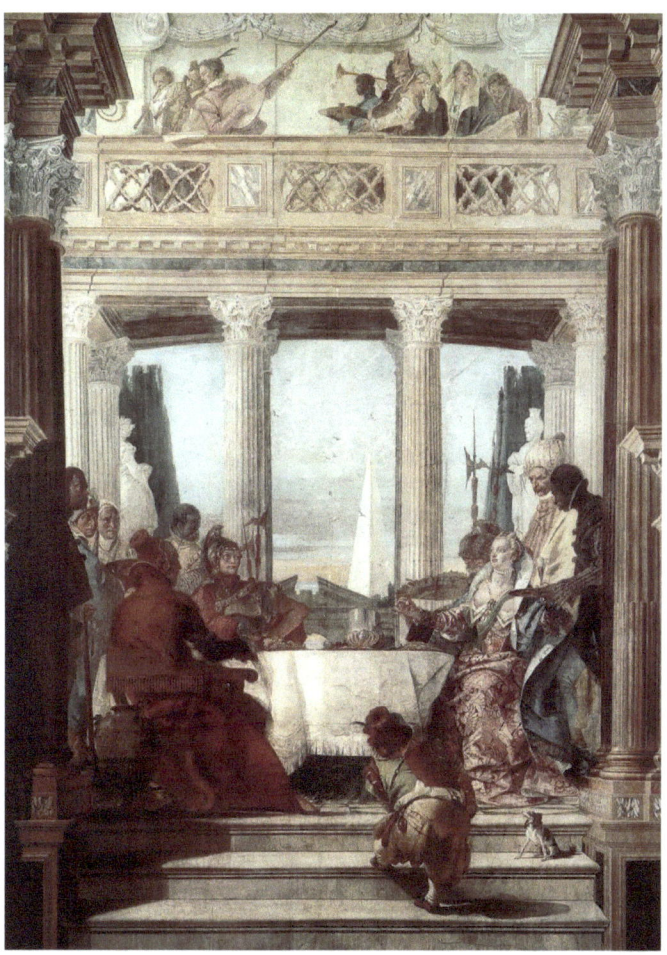

Next page: above, Raphael, *Expulsion of Heliodorus from the Temple* (on the left Pope Julius II), 1512, Vatican
Below: Parmigianino, *Parable of the Wise and Foolish Virgins* (detail), 1531-1539, Madonna della Steccata, Parma

Above: G.B. Tiepolo, *Banquet of Cleopatra*, 1746-1747, Palazzo Labia, Venice

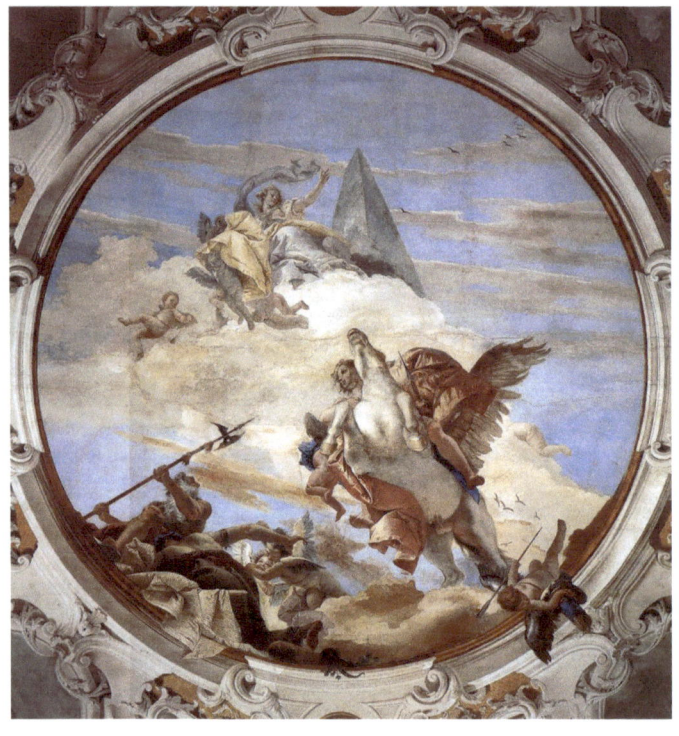

G.B. Tiepolo, *Bellerophon on Pegasus*, 1746–1747, Palazzo Labia, Venice

Body and Soul

Fresco painting had a triple function: to instruct, entertain and move the viewer. The painter's prime task was to get across the message of the painting. For the painting was meant to edify the viewer. But it was not enough to convey the message in a plain, straightforward way. The painter had to present it in an appealing manner and to entertain and surprise the viewer with clever details and a variety of postures and movements. An effective way of doing this was by including one or more figures who fulfilled a role comparable to that of the chorus in Greek theatre. Their task was to engage the viewer and clarify what happening, by raising their hand to catch their attention or making gestures to get them to laugh or cry. When the viewer feels involved, he is more likely to be receptive to the message. Above all, a painting had to have the power to deeply move the viewer. Painting is primarily about arousing emotions in the viewer. The artist had to create personages that the viewer can empathise with, so that they in turn 'weep, laugh and grieve' with them. A painter who could create beings of flesh and blood was himself a god among men, almost God's equal. He was the progeny of the legendary artist Pygmalion who fell in love with a statue he had made and which magically came to life. Boccaccio breathed new life into the classic Pygmalion myth. In one of his stories in *The Decameron* he describes Giotto as a painter in whose work 'everything he painted was more like the real thing than a representation'. Boccaccio ushered in a new standard for judging painting. 'Lifelike' was no longer merely taken to mean 'well reproduced', but rather that a work of art should actually have a soul. Writers tripped over themselves to find words to describe 'lifelike' in the new sense. According to Vasari the frescoes of Raphael were 'not paintings, but living creations, for the flesh of his figures is alive, one sees their minds and their violent emotions, one is conscious of reality itself.' A whole gamut of standard expressions to this effect were coined for praising a work of art: 'all that is wanting is the figure's voice', or even stronger: 'how is it possible that his voice has not yet been heard', 'a figure so lifelike that he resembles a person of flesh and blood', a portrait 'so well captured that it seems to breathe', 'everything here seems to speak, despite the silence'. Finally, 'a figure more real than reality itself', and of course its opposite, a representation of the dead Christ, 'more dead than death itself'.

How did a painter manage to convey the endless diversity of interior emotions, the *accidenti mentali*, to the public? For one thing, he could draw on conventional gesture language. In the fresco of *Christ before the High Priest* in the Scrovegni Chapel in Padua the priest tears his robe from his breast. The meaning of this gesture can be deciphered with the help of the personification of virtues and vices that Giotto painted in *grisaille* below his scenes of the *Pas-*

sion of the Christ. In this, the personification of anger, *Ira*, makes the same gesture as the high priest. This gesture is therefore an expression of his wrath (pl. p. 103).

But gestures alone were not enough for a scene to move the viewer. The whole body language including the facial expression had to project emotion. And thanks to their increasing technical command of their metier, the painters were equipped to do so. Giotto and his contemporaries had a limited number of standard facial expressions at their disposal, no more than three or four, nowhere near enough to cover the virtually infinite variety of facial expressions in real life. Two centuries later it was a very different situation. The faces are aglow with life and betray every shade of emotion. And that, wrote Alberti, while anyone who has ever tried knows how hard it is not to create a sad expression when you try to paint a happy one, or how difficult it is to paint a face in which the lips, chin, eyes, cheeks, forehead and eyebrows combine to express sorrow or joy.

The portrayal of interior motives was based on a profound study of the connection between body and soul. Leonardo da Vinci, the first great painter of the soul, made this the keystone of his artistic programme. He studied the deaf and dumb as well as orators to grasp the meaning behind a gesture, and on more than one occasion he followed an expressive individual around all day with his sketchbook, making notes on his postures as he talked, quarrelled, or joked. His search for the connection between body and soul resulted in the enormous concentration of expressive postures, gestures and facial expressions that made his *Last Supper* such a revolutionary work of art (pl. p. 40). The *Last Judgment* in the Sistine Chapel likewise owes its fame to the fact that Michelangelo presents the whole spectrum of man's inner and outer being. Vasari described the fresco as 'filled with every possible human mood, each one admirably expressed, for the haughty, the envious, the voluptuous and all the other sinners, can easily be distinguished by a discerning mind, because in all his figures Michelangelo respected decorum, both regarding their facial expressions as well as their postures, and in every other matter concerned.' (pl. p. 104) And he had succeeded in doing so, according to Vasari, because his genius and experience had led him to the same insights as the philosophers had acquired from contemplation and the scriptures.

Quoted Sources

ALBERTI, Leon Battista, *De Pictura*, 1435 (*Della Pittura*, 1436).
English edition:
ALBERTI, Leon Battista, *On Painting*, Cambridge University Press, 2011.
BELLORI, Giovanni Pietro, *Vite de'pittori, scultori et architetti moderni*, 1672.
English edition:
BELLORI, G.P., *The lives of the Modern Painters, Sculptors and Architects*, Cambridge, 2005.
BORGHINI, Raffaello, *Il Riposo*, 1584.
CASTIGLIONE, Baldassare, *Il libro del Cortegiano*, Venezia, 1528.
English edition:
CASTIGLIONE, B., *The Book of the Courtier,* New York, 2008.
CENNINO d'Andrea Cennini da Colle di Val d'Elsa, *Il libro dell'Arte*, c. 1410.
English edition:
CENNINO, *The Craftman's Handbook*, Yale University Press, 1933, reprint of the English translation, Dover Publications, New York, 1960.

CONDIVI, Ascanio, *Vita di Michelanguolo Buonarroti*, Roma, 1553.
English edition:
CONDIVI, Ascanio, *The life of Michelangelo*, Pennsylvania University Press, 1976.
DOMINICI, Bernardo de, *Vita del Cavaliere D. Luca Giordano, pittore Napoletano*, Napoli, 1729.
HOLANDA, Francisco de, *Da Pintura antiga*, (tom. II) *Diálogos de Roma*, Lisbon, 1548.
LEONARDO DA VINCI, *Trattato della Pittura*, first publication 1651 by Raffaelo du Fresne, Paris.
English edition:
A Treatise on Painting by Leonardo da Vinci, London, 2004
LOMAZZO, Gian Paolo, *Trattato dell'arte della pittura, scoltura et architettura*, Milano, 1585.
PONTORMO, Jacopo, *Il libro mio* (National Library, Florence), 1554-1556.
English edition:
Pontormo's Diary, London, 1979.
POZZO, Andrea, *Perspectiva pictorum et architectorum*, Roma, 2 vols., 1693-1700.
English edition:
POZZO, Andrea, *Perspective in architecture and painting*, New York, Dover Publication, 1989.
VASARI, Giorgio, *Le vite de' più eccelenti architetti, pittori, et scultori italiani, de Cimabue insino a' tempi nostri*, 1550-1558.
English edition:
VASARI, Giorgio, *The Lives of the Artists*, Oxford, 1998.

Chronological Overview

Period 1290-1400

Until approximately 1250 major figurative art commissions are realised in mosaic and not in fresco. The roles are reversed when an important church as the San Francesco in Assisi is completely decorated with fresco. Fresco proves a more suitable medium than mosaic for depicting narrative scenes, which serve as an aid to preaching, one of the Franciscan monks' main tasks. The frescoes are executed by painters from Rome, Siena and Florence. Together they pave the way for the development of Italian fresco art.

Themes

Initially, most frescoes portray devotional themes. Later, though, the emphasis shifts to narrative paintings, cycles of which form a continuous story. In addition to traditional biblical tales, themes are taken from the lives of the saints, large numbers of which are published at this time. Apocryphal tales, such as those related in the medieval best-seller, The Golden Legend *(Legenda Aurea)* by Jacopo da Voragine, are another source of inspiration. Apocryphal tales include episodes from the lives of Maria and her parents, Joachim and Anna, and these are regularly depicted in fresco cycles.

Besides the devotional and anecdotal scenes there is a third genre: the allegory. Large allegorical fresco cycles of encyclopaedic scope are found in both secular and religious settings. Examples of these two categories are respectively *Good and Bad Government* in the Palazzo Pubblico in Siena and the *Via Veritatis* and the allegory of Christian doctrine in the Chapter House, the so-called Spanish Chapel of the monastery of Santa Maria Novella in Florence (pl. p. 106). Extensive paintings like these of abstract yet memorisable ideas in tandem with concrete examples are typical of the 14th century.

Composition

Scenes are arranged in two or three registers one above the other as in a comic (pl. p. 105, 42). On entering a church or chapel, the scenes usually begin in the top right-hand corner at the end of the nave and from there read horizontally from left to right and from top to bottom. The composition of the individual scenes is adapted to the horizontal direction in which they are read. The action takes place in the foreground. The background or backdrop is usually little more than a schematic indication of the location and serves merely to reinforce the meaning and expressivity of the scene in the foreground. The scenes are therefore primarily two-dimensional in character.

In the second half of the 14th century *horror vacui* results in crowded compositions.

Figures

Until c. 1300 human figures are painted in Byzantine style, i.e., based on a largely fixed scheme and the principle that the more important the figure, the larger they are portrayed.

After 1300, the figures are more or less naturally proportioned and rendered plastically through the use of light and shade. Postures and gestures indicate their inner feelings.

Backdrop

The main purpose of the background is to spatially isolate the events enacted in the foreground rather than to offer a view of the hinterland or surroundings. Spatially therefore there is no correlation between the foreground and background. Landscapes are no more than rockwork props that reproduce the contours of the figures in the foreground. Here and there trees and buildings are symbolically represented. Interior scenes are viewed from the outside as if the exterior wall has been removed as in a doll's house (pl. p. 103 above).

Ornamentation

Fresco painters are responsible for the complete decoration of the walls and vaults of a chapel. In practice, this leaves a lot of places to be decorated that do not lend themselves to narrative painting, such as portals, vault ribs and panelwork. Like the frames of the narrative scenes, these residual spaces are adorned with decorative painting, imparting a sense of opulence to the chapel or room. Very often these are decorated with feigned materials and techniques: marble inlay work, mosaics, marble slabs, damask curtains or marble statues painted in *grisaille* (pl. p. 103 below). The repetitive character of the ornamentation produces a continuous bourdon tone that throws the main scenes into relief. The visual idiom is gothic: pointed arches, four-partite medallions, flower motifs.

Period 1400-1500

Besides public bodies such as the church, guilds, and city councils, wealthy citizens and local princes commission major art projects: the Medici family in Florence, the Montefeltro in Urbino, the Gonzaga in Mantua, the D'Este in Ferrara, and the Sforza in Milan.

This period, the Renaissance, saw a major revival of interest in classical antiquity. Classical art and art theories inspire the pursuit of 'selective realism', the replication of reality purged of offensive or trivial elements.

Themes

The themes are by and large the same as those of the preceding period: devotional and anecdotal images, borrowed from the Bible, the lives of saints and the Golden Legend. Independent allegorical fresco cycles, however, are rare. Patrons and their retinue are prominently featured in the frescoes, irrespective of the place or time of action. In family chapels patrons are generally positioned at eye level, on either side of the altar.

Inspired by classic antiquity, the 'famous men' (*uomini famosi*) genre gains ground. These are fictitious portraits of men (and sometimes women) from antiquity, the Bible and even later eras (Dante, Petrarch). A cognate genre are the frescoes glorifying family dynasties: the *Camera degli*

Sposi, Palazzo Ducale Mantua and the *Sala dei Mesi*, Palazzo Schifanoia, Ferrara, serve the greater glory of respectively the Gonzaga and the D'Este families.

Composition

Painters strive to link the individual scenes of their fresco cycles. Instead of a succession of isolated tableaux, these are now presented as a continuous cycle of stories. Each fresco depicts several events, or else the events are enacted behind a continuous colonnade. This is a transitional period which prepares the way for a novel application of fresco decoration as an illusory extension of real space (pl. p. 108 above).

Sometimes painters opt for a thematic as opposed to chronological arrangement of the scenes. In such cases, related themes are depicted at the same height on facing walls, as in the case of the *Finding of the True Cross* by Piero della Francesca in Arezzo (pl. p. 44, 45).

The composition within each individual scene consists in the symmetrical arrangement of figures on either side of a central motif (triangular compositions, pl. p. 97). This results in static groups of figures in the first half of the 15th century. Later compositions are freer and more varied.

Figures

Inspired by classical sculpture, there is a sudden increase in the depiction of nudes. Painters train by sketching from naked models, copying classical statues and, toward the close of the 15th century, in some instances by dissecting corpses. In the early 15th century nudes are represented with anatomical accuracy, but in less detail than when painters are able to differentiate between muscle, bone and veins (pl. p. 101 below). In the early years painters tended to confine themselves to a static representation. If they were required to paint figures in action, they relied heavily on fluttering robes to compensate for the woodenness of their movements (as in the work of Ghirlandaio, pl. p. 108 below).

Backdrop

The most important development in Renaissance painting is the discovery of linear perspective. This enables painters to convincingly evoke a sense of depth in their backdrop. Objects and people are systematically downsized the farther back they stand. Following the discovery of linear perspective, fresco paintings feature an abundance of tiled floors, as an aid to the construction of the perspective (pl. p. 98 above).

The eye of the viewer, which in earlier frescoes focused on the foreground, is now drawn deeper into the painting. The backdrop, which had hitherto merely supported the main action, now suddenly plays a major role in the painting. The symbolic indication of location makes way for realistic-looking landscapes and urban scenery. Typical of this era is the incorporation of many classical monuments, statues and ornaments in a contemporary setting (pl. p. 108 below).

Ornamentation

Ornaments are integrated into the main scenes. Decorative frames are replaced by columns or pillars painted according to the same principles of perspective as the main subject. Sometimes they recur elsewhere in the picture, resized in perspective. Many ornaments are included as *trompe l'oeil* elements: feigned painted curtains or tapestries, hanging over the edge of the painting and the like.

Gothic ornaments are replaced by those of the Renaissance: classical colonnades, cornices, cartouches. Highly popular from the last quarter of the 15th century are the *grotesques* that are borrowed from the painted ornaments in Nero's then recently excavated Golden House (pl. p. 109 below).

Period 1500-1600

Rome becomes the cultural centre of Italy with the Pope as most important patron. Michelangelo paints the Sistine Chapel (vault 1508-1512, *Last Judgement* 1534-1541), Raphael, the papal rooms and loggias of the Vatican. With the exception of Michelangelo's *Last Judgement*, after the plundering of Rome (*Sacco di Roma*), the Papal court commissions no further major fresco cycles.

Frescoes are no longer commissioned for the sole purpose of conveying a message, but mainly for their unique artistic value, and the prestige of the maker. In this age of Mannerism, the artist's virtuosity and originality are highly-rated qualities. The principle of art for art's sake is practiced long before the expression *l'art pour l'art* is coined in the 19th century.

Themes

Traditional biblical themes tend to be rendered in a free and unorthodox manner and are interlaced with elements from pagan antiquity. Frescoes commissioned by the Pope frequently contain a hidden propagandistic message. Biblical or historical images are often assigned a contemporary significance by endowing the protagonists with the features of the patron (pl. p. 107, 110 above). Following the Council of Trent (1545-1563), which heralded the start of the Counter-Reformation, the church strictly monitors the responsible iconographical representation of Christian themes. The depiction of nudes is restricted, sexual organs are concealed from view. Nudes in earlier frescoes are furnished with loin cloths or fig leaves. Many apocryphal stories (like those from the Golden Legend) are scrapped from the standard repertory. In secular settings, however, there is an increasing demand for overt erotic painting (Giulio Romano, Palazzo del Te, Mantua).

Composition

Fresco cycles form a coherent whole. Each scene covers a whole wall. In some instances, all the paintings on the walls and vault are devoted to a single subject. The events appear to take place before the viewer's eyes, giving the viewer a sense of involvement (pl. p. 47).

In contrast with the serene, harmonious arrangement of figures in the early Renaissance, compositions now combine empty space with areas crowded with figures. In this way, the painter adds tension and emotion to the painting.

Figures

Painters break free of the classical principles governing the relative proportions of the human body. They create supermen with unnaturally elongated and graceful limbs (pl. p. 110 below) or figures who are broad and bulky with incredible bundles of muscle. They also pursue maximum movement and diversity of posture. Characteristic for this period is the elegantly spiralling posture that was introduced by Michelangelo, the *figura serpentinata*. In this posture, the front, back and profile are visible at the same time. The neck and shoulders turn in different directions, creating a dramatic, dynamic effect. By rendering figures on a flat wall three-dimensionally, the painter vies with the sculptor who is able to portray a figure from all sides. (pl. p. 102).

Thanks to his technical mastery of the human anatomy, the painter is now able to express emotion in gesticular and body language. He is admired if his figures are not only life-like but also show their emotions so that 'all that is wanting is the figure's voice'.

Backdrop

The painted space is an illusory extension of real space. Either the painted floor patterns, columns, consoles and cornices are constructed in perspective to correspond exactly with the actual location (pl. p. 46 below) or the viewer looks out over an idyllic landscape from behind a painted balcony or pergola. The dividing line between reality and illusion is blurred. The viewer is drawn into the world of the fresco. In turn, the painting invades the viewer's space, for instance, when figures are strongly foreshortened and arms and legs appear to dangle over the edge of the painting.

Ornamentation

Ornaments are now fully integrated in the painting. Decorative elements, such as festoons and medallions, no longer surround the fresco but form an integral part of it (pl. p. 48).

After 1600

The main commissions for fresco painters are for the decoration of halls and reception rooms in palazzi and villas, or the painting of church cupolas. Fresco art generally loses some of its importance. This is due in part to the growing commercialisation of art and the rise of the art trade and art cabinets, which stimulates the demand for movable art, such as panel paintings. Frescoes are obviously not collector's items. Ironically, it is in and around Venice, where fresco art had traditionally commanded the least attention, that Italian fresco art last blossoms, in the 18th century. It is here that Giambattista Tiepolo (1696-1770) works, who later in his career exports Italy's fresco tradition abroad and is active in Würzburg as well as in Madrid.

Themes

Following the Council of Trent, a sharp distinction is made between religious and secular art. In churches, art is inspired by Christian iconography; in the halls of the palazzi and villas by mythological or literary scenes.

The number of narrative scenes in churches rapidly declines. The emphasis shifts to scenes of an apotheotic nature, with tremendous visions of Heaven and ascensions of recent saints, such as Ignatius de Loyola or Carlo Borromeo (pl. p. 100).

In secular circles, we find almost exclusively images derived from classical and neo-classical literature and mythology (pl. p. 48)). The mythological scenes in the wealthy mansions and villas often have an allegorical meaning.

They contain subtle, erudite references to the merits, fame and honour of the family. In the 18th century, the solemnity of these paintings is relieved as the painters incorporate playful *trompe l'oeil* effects and witty, everyday details (pl. p. 111, 132). In these paintings allegory, mythology and everyday reality interfuse.

Composition

Frescoes form part of a strictly orchestrated total work in which architecture, interior design, sculpture and painting are coordinated. In the churches frescoes are now mainly applied to vaulted cupolas. Because of the distance from which they are viewed, the images are chiefly made up of large planes of lights and darks. Painted architecture (*quadratura*) also plays an important structural role. When depicting two or more levels of reality or secondary scenes, the painter creates either mock panel paintings within the fresco (so-called *quadri riportati)* or medallions on which he depicts scenes of a different nature in *grisaille* or fake bronze.

Figures

Since frescoes are now viewed from a great distance, the figures no longer need distinguishing facial features. The artist tended to confine himself to emphatic gestures and uplifted eyes. In secular settings, the powerful emotions of (nude) figures are legible in the tensed muscles and contorted postures.

Figures in the vault paintings are portrayed with extreme foreshortening in the line of sight of the viewer below (*di sotto in su*). The figures either approach the viewer (*putti* dangling their legs over cornices, figures diving down, pl.

p. 112) or they are whisked away from him in a dynamic upward ascent only to dissolve in a heavenly golden radiance.

Backdrop

Church vaults and cupolas are transformed into a radiant golden heaven; clouds floating in lower spheres gradually blend into the glow above. Painted architecture (*quadratura*) is often the work of specialists (pl. p. 111). Staircases, balconies and strongly foreshortened columns, visually double the actual height of the church and lead the eye up to heaven.

Ornamentation

The painted *trompe-l'oeil* elements collude with the stucco decorations to keep the viewer guessing as to where reality ends and illusion begins.

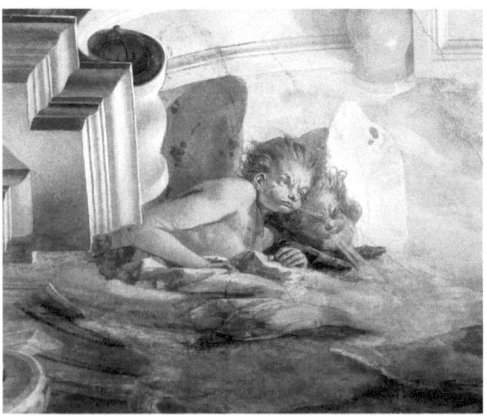

G.B. Tiepolo, *The Wind* (detail), Palazzo Labia, Venice

Frescoes according to region

North West Italy
Valle d'Aosta-Piedmont-Liguria

Aosta, Sant'Orso, early 11C frescoes in the roof vaulting.

Chieri, Duomo, Battistero, Guglielmo Fantini, fresco cycle of the Passion, 1430

Genoa, Cathedral, main portal, 14C frescoes, nave and presbytery 16-17C works by Luca Cambiaso, Federico Barocci, Giovanni Andrea Ansaldo and Lazzaro Tavarone.

Genoa, SS Annunziata del Vastato, cupola, Andrea Ansaldo, Assumption, 1635-1638.

Genoa, Palazzo Balbi-Senarega, Sala delle Rovine, Gregorio de Ferrari, decorative frescoes, 1684.

Genoa, Villa Pallavicino della Peschiere, Cambiaso and 'Il Bergamasco', mythological and pastoral scenes, mid 16C.

Genoa, Palazzo del Principe, Perin del Vaga, Mythological scenes and Roman history, 1529-1533.

Issogne, Castello Challant, loggia, Scenes of everyday life, c.1490-1502.

Manta, Castello di Manta, Giacomo Jaquerio, Fountain of Youth, heroes and heroines, 1418-1430.
Novara, Duomo, Cappella San Siro, Romanesque frescoes, 12-13C.
Novara, Battistero, frescoes of the Apocalypse, 10-11C.
Varallo, Sacro Monte, 45 chapels with frescoes of Life and Passion of Christ, 16C.
Varallo, Santa Maria delle Grazie, Gaudenzio Ferrari, Life of Christ, 1513.
Vercelli, San Cristoforo, Gaudenzio Ferrari, Stories of the Virgin Mary, 1529-1534.
Vigevano, Ducal residence, Hunting scenes,1466-1476.

North East Italy
Trentino Alto Adige-Veneto-Friuli

Bergamo, Santa Maria Maggiore, Ciro Ferri, cycle of biblical scenes, 1665-1667.
Bergamo, Trescore, Oratorio Suardi, Lorenzo Lotto, Christ and legends of saints, 1523-1524
Bergamo, San Michele al Pozzo Bianco, 12-14C frescoes and Lorenzo Lotto, Life of the Virgin Mary, 1525
Castello Roganzuolo (Conegliano), Chiesa dei Santi Pietro e Paolo, Francesco da Milano, Life of the saints Peter and Paul, 1525.
Conegliano, Sala dei Battuti, external façade, Ludovico Pozzoserrato, Scenes of the Old Testament, 1593; interior, Francesco da Milano, Scenes of the New Testament, 1511.
Malles Venosta (Bolzano), San Benedetto, portrait of feudal lord, 9C.

Maser, Villa Barbaro, Paolo Veronese, Allegorical and trompe-l'oeuil paintings, 1560-1561.

Padua, Cappella Scrovegni, Giotto, Life of the Virgin Mary, Passion of Christ, Last Judgment and allegorical scenes, about 1305.

Padua, Chiesa degli Eremitani, cappella Ovetari, Andrea Mantegna, Lives of the saints James and Christopher, 1448-1457.

Padua, Palazzo della Ragione, Salone Grande, fresco cycle of astrological scenes and various professions, 1425-1440.

Padua, Battistero, Giusto de'Menabuoi, Christ Pantocrator, Genesis, lives of Christ and John the Baptist; in the apse Visions of the Apocalypse, about 1380.

Padua, Sant'Antonio di Padova, Altichiero, Cappella di San Giacomo, Story of St .James and Crucifixion, 1376-1379.

Padua, Scuola del Santo, Titian, Stories of Saint Anthony of Padua, 1511.

Padua, Oratorio di San Giorgio, Altichiero da Zevio, and Jacopo Avanzo, Stories of Christ and the saints George, Catherine and Lucy, 1379-1384.

Pinzolo, San Vigilio, external fresco by Simone II Baschenis, Dance of Death, 1539.

San Pietro di Feletto (Treviso), outer portal, Sunday Christ, nave and aisles, biblical scenes 12-15C; apse, Christ Pantocrator 13C, Cappella San Sebastiano, c. 1470.

Stra, Villa Pisani, G. B. Tiepolo, Apotheosis of the family Pisani, 1761-1762.

Trento, Castello del Buonconsiglio (Torre dell'Aquila), Cycle of the Months, early 15C; in the Palazzo Magno fresco decorations of Dosso Dossi and Girolamo Romanino, early 16C.

Treviso, Santa Caterina, Tommaso da Modena, Life of Saint Ursula, about 1350.

Treviso, San Niccolò, Chapter House, Tommaso da Modena, Portraits of monks (with the earliest depiction of eyeglasses), 1352.

Udine, Palazzo Arcivescovile, frescoes by G. B. Tiepolo: on the stairs, Fall of the Angels, Gallery and Sala Rossa, Scenes of the Old Testament, 1726-1730.

Udine, Oratorio della Purità, ceiling Giambattista Tiepolo, Assumption; on the walls monochrome allegorical and biblical scenes by Giandomenico Tiepolo, 1759.

Udine, Duomo, Bell Tower, frescoes by Vitale da Bologna, 1349.

Udine, Santa Maria di Castello, Deposition and the Apostles, 13C.

Venice, Palazzo Labia, Salone, G. B. Tiepolo and Mengozzi Colonna, Banquet of Cleopatra, 1746.

Venice, La Pietà, ceiling of the nave, G. B. Tiepolo, Triumph of Faith, 1762.

Venice, Ca' Rezzonico, frescoes of Villa di Zianigo by Giovanni Battista and Giandomenico Tiepolo, 1759.

Venice, Santa Maria del Rosario (Gesuati), ceiling frescoes by G. B. Tiepolo, Institution of the Rosary, 1737-1739.

Verona, Sant'Anastasia, Cappella Pellegrini, Pisanello, Saint George and the Princess, 1437-1438; Cappella Cavalli, Altichiero, Adoration of the Virgin Mary, last quarter 14C.

Verona, San Fermo, Pisanello, Annunciation (on the funeral monument of Nicolò di Brenzoni), 1426.

Verona, Santa Maria in Organo, vast fresco decoration by Francesco Morone and others, early 16C.

Vicenza, Villa Valmarana, Giovanni Battista Tiepolo, scenes from the Iliad of Homer, Aeneid of Virgil, Orlando Furioso by Ariosto and Gerusalemme liberata by Tasso; Foresteria, rural scenes by Giandomenico Tiepolo, 1757.

Lombardy and Emilia-Romagna

Bologna, San Giacomo Maggiore, Cappella Bentivoglio, Lorenzo Costa, The Apocalypse, Triumph of Death and Madonna enthroned, 1483.

Bologna, San Giacomo Maggiore, Oratorio di Santa Cecilia, Lorenzo Costa, Francesco Francia and Amico Aspertini, Legends of St. Cecilia and St. Valerian, 1504-1506.

Bologna, San Petronio, Cappella Bolognini, Giovanni da Modena, Last Judgment, Life of San Petronio and the Magi, about 1410.

Bologna, Palazzo Poggi (University), Pellegrino Tibaldi, Stories of Ulysses, 1555; on the piano nobile, landscapes, mythological and biblical scenes by Niccolo dell'Abate and Prospero Fontana.

Castelseprio, Santa Maria Foris Portas, Cycle of the Nativity of Christ, 8 or 9 C.

Castiglione Olona, Battistero, Masolino da Panicale, Life of John the Baptist, 1435.

Castiglione Olona, Collegiata, Masolino da Panicale, Life of the Virgin Mary, about1435.

Cremona, Sant'Agata, Giulio Campi, sanctuary walls, Life of St Agatha, 1536.

Cremona, Duomo, fresco decorations nave and apse by Gian Francesco Bembo, Pordenone et al., 1524-1529.

Ferrara, Palazzo Schifanoia, Salone dei Mesi, Cosimo Tura, Francesco del Cossa, Ercole de' Roberti, Cycle of the Zodiac and the rule of duke Borso d'Este, 1466-1470.

Ferrara, Sant'Antonio in Polesine, School of Giotto, Life of the Virgin Mary and the Passion, 14C.

Mantua, Palazzo Ducale, Camera degli Sposi, Andrea Mantegna, Ludovico Gonzaga and his family, 1465-1474.

Mantua, Palazzo Te, Sala di Psyche, Giulio Romano, Story of Psyche; Camera da Letto, Fall of Phaeton; Sala dei Giganti, Fall of the giants, 1525-1530.

Mantua, Palazzo d'Arco, Giovanni Maria Falconetto, Cycle of the Zodiac, early 16C.

Milan, Castello Sforzesco, Leonardo da Vinci, decoration Sala delle Asse, about 1495.

Milan, Palazzo Dugnani, Giambattista Tiepolo, Salone del Tiepolo, Allegorical scenes, 1731.

Milan, Santa Maria delle Grazie, refectory, Leonardo da Vinci, Last Supper (Cenacolo), 1495-1498.

Milan, San Maurizio, Bernardo Luini, Life of San Maurizio and Life of St. Catherine, 1522-1529.

Milan, San Pietro in Gessate, Bernardino Butinone and Bernardo Zenale, Cappella Grifi, Life of St. Ambrose, 1491-1493.

Milan, San Simpliciano, apse, Ambrogio Bergognone, Coronation of the Virgin Mary, 1524.

Monza, San Giovanni Battista, workshop Zavatarri, Legend of queen Theodelinda, 1444.

Parma, Camera di San Paolo, Correggio, Mythological and allegorical scenes, 1519; also frescoes by Alessandro Araldi, 1514.
Parma, Duomo, dome, Correggio, Assumption of the Virgin, 1524.
Parma, Battistero, 13C frescoes on vault and lunettes.
Parma, San Giovanni Evangelista, dome, Correggio, Vision of John on Patmos; lunette above door to sacristy: St. John and the eagle; nave frieze with monochrome frescoes, 1520/1521; first two chapels (left), frescoes by Parmigianino.
Parma, Madonna della Steccata, dome, Bernardo Gatti, Assumption of the Virgin, Parmigianino, the Wise and Foolish Virgins, 1531-1539.
Parma, Fontanellato, Rocca Sanvitale, Parmigianino, Story of Diana and Actaeon, 1524.
Parma (prov.) *San Secondo,* Rocca dei Rossi, Sala dei Gesta Rossiana, Cesare Baglione and Ercole Procaccini, Scenes from the Golden Ass by Apuleius and Aesop's Fables, about 1570.
Pavia, Certosa di, various frescoes by Ambrogio Bergognone, 1486-1494.
Pavia, San Teodoro, Bernardino Lanzani, View of Pavia, 1524.
Piacenza, Duomo, dome, frescoes by Morazzone and Guercino, 1626; nave, frescoes by Camillo Procaccini and Ludovico Carracci, 16C
Piacenza, Madonna di Campagna, dome frescoes by Pordenone and Bernardino Gatti, 1530-1532.
Pomposa abbey, apse, frescoes by Vitale da Bologna, mid 14C; early 14C frescoes in the Chapter House and refectory.

140   FRESCOES ACCORDING TO REGION

Rimini, Tempio Malatestiano (San Francesco), Piero della Francesca, Sigismondo Malatesta kneeling before St. Sigismund, 1451.
Torrechiara (prov. Parma), Castello, Camera d'Oro, Benedetto Bembo, Bianca Pellegrini running her and Rossi's fiefs, searching for her lover, about 1460.

Tuscany

Arezzo, San Francesco, chancel, Piero della Francesca, Legend of the True Cross, vault by Bicci di Lorenzo, mid 15C.
Arezzo, Duomo, next to the door of the sacristy, Piero della Francesca, Mary Magdalene, 1460.
Empoli, Santo Stefano, Masolino da Panicale, Sant' Ivo and Madonna with Child, 1424.
Empoli, Museo della Collegiata di Sant'Andrea, Pietà, 1424.
Florence, Santa Maria del Fiore (Duomo), Above main door, Paolo Uccello, clock with four heads of prophets; left aisle, Andrea del Castagno, equestrian monument of Nicolò da Tolentino (1456), Uccello, equestrian monument of Sir John Hawkwood (1436); dome, Last Judgment by Vasari and Zuccari, 1572-1576.
Florence, Palazzo Vecchio, Sala dei Gigli, Cappella di Eleonora, frescoes di Bronzino, 1545, Domenico Ghirlandaio, Famous men and Roman emperors, 1482-1484.
Florence, Santa Croce, chancel, Agnolo Gaddi, Legend of the True Cross; Cappella Bardi, Giotto, Life of Francis of Assisi, Cappella Peruzzi, Lives of John the Baptist and St. John Evangelist; Cappella Baroncelli, Tad-

deo Gaddi, Life of the Virgin Mary; Cappella Bardi di Vernio, Maso di Banco, Life of St. Silvestre; Cappella Castellani, Agnolo Gaddi, Stories of St. Nicholas; Cappella Rinuccini, Giovanni da Milano, Lives of the Virgin Mary and Mary Magdalene. Museo dell' Opera di S. Croce (fomerly refectory), Taddeo Gaddi, Last Supper and Genealogical Tree, 1335-1340.

Florence, Santa Maria Novella, chancel, Domenico Ghirlandaio, Lives of John the Baptist and the Virgin Mary, 1486-1490; Cappella Filippo Strozzi, Filippino Lippi, Lives of St. John the Evangelist and St. Philip; Cappella Strozzi, Orcagna and Nardo di Cione, Last Judgment, Hell and Paradise, 1355-1360; Left aisle, Masaccio, Holy Trinity, 1427. Chiostro verde, Paolo Uccello, scenes of Genesis, 1445; Chapter (Spanish Chapel), Andrea da Firenze (Andrea di Bonaiuto), Allegories of the Dominican order and Crucifixion, about1365.

Florence, Santa Trinità, Cappella Sassetti, Domenico Ghirlandaio, Life of Francis of Assisi and donors,1482-1485.

Florence, Ognissanti, Domenico Ghirlandaio, Madonna della Misericordia: Saint Jerome; Botticelli, St. Augustine. Refectory: Ghirlandaio, Last Supper, about 1480.

Florence, San Marco, Chapter, Fra Angelico, allegorical scenes. Corridor and cells, biblical scenes, 1436-1445; Refectory, Domenico Ghirlandaio, Last Supper, 1482.

Florence, SS. Annunziata, Chiostrino dei Voti, Pontormo, Rosso Fiorentino, Andrea del Sarto, Franciabigio, Cosimo Rosselli, Baldovinetti, scenes of the Bible and Apocryphical books; left aisle, Andrea del Castagno, Vision of St. Jerome, 1455.

Florence Sant'Apollonia, Andrea del Castagno, Last Supper and scenes from the Passion of Christ, about 1447. Paolo Schiavo, Crucifixion, about 1440.

Florence, Palazzo Medici-Riccardi, Chapel, Benozzo Gozzoli, Journey of the Magi, 1459-1461.

Florence, Chiostro dello Scalzo, Andrea del Sarto, monochrome frescoes, Life of John the Baptist, 1520-1526.

Florence, Santa Maria Maddalena dei Pazzi, Chapter House, Perugino, Crucifixion, 1493-1496.

Florence, Santo Spirito, Refectory, Orcagna, Crucifixion, mid 14C.

Florence, Santa Maria del Carmine, Cappella Brancacci, Masolino da Panicale and Masaccio (1423-1428), Fillipino Lippi (1481-1485), Adam and Eve, Stories of St. Peter and St. Paul.

Florence, Palazzo Pitti, Palatine Gallery, Pietro da Cortona, Astrological and mythological scenes, 1637 and 1643-1647.

Florence, San Miniato, sacristy, Spinello Aretino, Life of St. Benedict, 1387-1388.

Florence, Certosa Galluzzo, Jacopo Pontormo, The Passion of Christ, 1523-1525.

Florence, San Salvi, Andrea del Sarto, Last Supper, about 1520-1525.

Florence, Villa Poggio a Caiano, Salone, Glory and Virtue of the House of Medici by Franciabigio, Andrea del Sarto, Alessandro Allori, Lunette: Vertumnus and Pomona by Pontormo, 1519-1521.

Lucca, San Frediano, Cappella Sant'Agostino, Amico Aspertini, Lives of St. Augustine and San Frediano; story of the Volto Santo, 1508-1509.
Monte Oliveto, abbey, Chiostro grande, Luca Signorelli and Il Sodoma, Life of St. Benedict, 1505-1508 and after 1513.
Monterchi, Piero della Francesca, Madonna del Parto, about 1460.
Pisa, Camposanto, Cloister, Benozzo Gozzoli, Scenes from the Old Testament; Antonio Veneziano and Andrea Buonaiuti, Life of St. Rainieri; Spinello Aretino, Life of St. Ephysius; Taddeo Gaddi, story of Job; Piero di Puccio, Theological Cosmography. Cappella Ammannati, Triumph of Death, Last Judgment, lives of the hermits, 1360-1380.
Pisa, Museo delle Sinopie: preparatory sketches for the frescoes of the Camposanto.
Marina di Pisa, San Piero a Grado, Deodato Orlandi, Life of St. Peter and portraits of popes, early 14C.
Prato, Duomo, chancel, Fra Filippo Lippi and Fra Diamante, Lives of St. Stephen and St. John the Baptist, 1452-1465.
San Gimignano, Sant'Agostino, chancel, Benozzo Gozzoli, Life of St. Augustine, 1464-1467.
San Gimignano, Collegiata, Cappella Santa Fina, Domenico Ghirlandaio, Life of Santa Fina, 1475-1478; right aisle, Barna da Siena or Lippo Memmi, scenes of the New Testament, left aisle, Bartolo di Fredi, Scenes of the Old Testament, 1356-1367; inner wall of the façade, Taddeo di Bartolo, Last Judgment, 1493; Gozzoli, St. Sebastian, 1465.

Sansepolcro, Pinacoteca (formerly Palazzo Comunale), Piero della Francesca, Resurrection, 1463.
Siena, Palazzo Pubblico, Sala del Mappamondo, Simone Martini, Maestà, 1315 and Guidoriccio da Fogliano at the siege of Montemassi; Sala della Pace, Ambrogio Lorenzetti, Allegory and the Effects of Good Government and Effects of Bad Government, 1338-1348.
Siena, Duomo, biblioteca Piccolomini, Pinturicchio, Life of Aeneas Silvius Piccolomini, 1502-1509.
Siena, San Francesco, left transept, Ambrogio Lorenzetti, Stories of the franciscans, Pietro Lorenzetti, Crucifixion, 1335-1340.
Siena, Ospedale Santa Maria della Scala, Pellegrinaio, Domenico di Bartolo, Lorenzo Vecchietta, Priamo della Quercia, History of the Spedale and Works of Mercy, 1440-1444.
Siena, Oratorio di San Bernardino, Gerolimo del Pacchia, Il Sodoma, Beccafumi, Life of the Virgin Mary, 1518-1532.
Siena, Santa Maria dei Servi, Pietro Lorenzetti, Slaughter of the Innocents, 1330-1340.

Umbria-Marches-Abruzzo-Molise

Assisi, San Francesco, Upper Church, Pietro Cavallini, Jacopo Torriti, Cimabue, Giotto, biblical scenes and Life of Francis of Assisi, 1290-1320.
Assisi, San Francesco, Lower Church, Cimabue, Giotto and school, Simone Martini (Cappella San Martino), Pietro Lorenzetti (left transept, Passion of Christ), Lives of saints and biblical scenes, 1290-1295, 1315-1320.

Atri, Santa Maria Assunta, chancel, Andrea de Litio, Lives of the Virgin Mary and Christ, about 1475.

Bominaco, Oratorio San Pellegrino, fresco cycle of biblical scenes and a liturgical calendar of feasts and signs of the zodiac, 13C.

Campi Vecchi (Norcia), pieve Santa Maria, Scenes of the Bible and the Apocryphical books, about 1400.

Capestrano, San Pietro ad Oratorium, Christ Pantocrator, early 12C.

Castel San Vincenzo, Badia di San Vincenzo, crypt, frescoes early 9C.

Ferentillo, San Pietro in Valle, Biblical scenes, end 12C.

Fossa, Santa Maria ad Cryptas, fresco cycle including Last Judgment, Life and Passion of Christ, and Months of the Year, 13C.

Fossacesia, San Giovanni in Venere, various frescoes in the apses, 12-13C.

Gubbio, Sant'Agostino, apse, Ottaviano Nelli, Life of St. Augustine and Last Judgment, early 15C.

Gubbio, San Francesco, Ottaviano Nelli, Stories of the Virgin Mary, 1408-1413.

Loreto, Santuario della Santa Casa, Sacristy San Giovanni, Luca Signorelli, Apostles, 1479; Sacristy San Marco, Melozzo da Forli, Angels with instruments of the Passion, Entry into Jerusalem, 1477-1480; Sala del Pomarancio, Pomarancio, Life of the Virgin Mary, 1605-1610.

Loreto Aprutino, Santa Maria in Piano, Last Judgment, Scenes of the New Testament and Life of St. Thomas Aquinas, 13-14C.

Montecosaro, Santa Maria a Piè di Chienti, Christ Pantocrator, 14-15C.

Montefalco, San Francesco, chancel, Benozzo Gozzoli, Life of Francis of Assisi, 1452.

Monte San Giusto, Palazzo Bonafede, allegorical frescoes by Amico Aspertini, ca. 1500.

Orvieto, Duomo, Cappella di San Brizio, Fra Angelico (vault, 1447), Luca Signorelli (1499-1504), Apocalypse, Acts of the Antichrist, Last Judgment, Hell and Paradise, 1499-1504.

Perugia, Collegio del Cambio, Sala di Udienza, Perugino, Famous men, Prophets and Sibyls, Nativity and Transfiguration of Christ, astrological scenes, 1496-1500.

Perugia, Palazzo del Consiglio, Benedetto Bonfigli, Lives of St. Louis of Toulouse and St. Herculanus, 1454.

Spello, Collegiata di Santa Maria Maggiore, Cappella Baglioni, Pinturicchio, Annunciation, Adoration of the shepherds, Christ among the doctors, 1500-1501.

Spoleto, Duomo Santa Maria, apse, Fra Filippo Lippi and Fra Diamante, Life of the Virgin Mary, 1466-1469; Cappella Eroli, frescoes by Pinturicchio.

Spoleto, Rocca, Camera Picta, Hunting scenes and scenes of courtly life, early 15C.

Tagliacozzo, San Francesco, cloister, Life of Francis of Assisi, 16C.

Todi, Duomo, above main entrance, Ferraù da Faenza, Last Judgment, 1594.

Tolentino, San Nicola, Cappellone di San Nicola, Life of St. Nicholas of Tolentino, 1330-1348.

Urbino, Oratorio San Giovanni Battista, Giacomo and Lorenzo Salimbeni, Life of St. John the Baptist, Crucifixion and votive paintings, about 1415.

Rome and Lazio

Anagni, Duomo, crypt, Cosmological scenes with Hippocrates and Galen, Visions of the Apocalypse, scenes of the Old Testament, mid 13C.

Arsoli, Castello Massimo, Federico and Taddeo Zuccari, Mythological scenes, 16C.

Caprarola, Villa Farnese, Zuccari brothers, Antonio Tempesta, Allegorical and mythological scenes glorifying the House Farnese, mid 16C.

Castel Sant'Elia, Basilica di Sant'Elia, chancel, frescoes 11-12C.

Grottaferrata, abbey Santa Maria, Domenichino, Life of St. Nilus, 1608.

Rome, Vatican palace, Cappella Niccolina, Fra Angelico, Lives of St. Stephen and St. Lawrence, 1448.

Rome, Vatican palace, Raphael Rooms, Stanza della Segnatura, Stanza di Eliodoro, Stanza dell' Incendio del Borgo, Stanza di Constantino, Raphael and assistants 1509-1514/1520.

Rome, Vatican palace, Raphael's Loggia, Biblical stories ('Raphael's Bible'), 1517.

Rome, Vatican palace, Appartamento Borgia, Sala dei Santi, Pinturicchio, Allegorical scenes, saints and prophets, biblical scenes, 1492-1495.

Rome, Sistine Chapel, on the walls Life of Moses and Life of Christ by Luca Signorelli, Perugino, Pinturicchio, Cosimo Rosselli, Sandro Botticelli, Domenico Ghirlandaio, about 1480; lunettes and ceiling, Michelangelo, ancestors of Christ, prophets and sibyls, nine scenes from the Book of Genesis, 1508-1512: sanctuary wall, Michelangelo, Last Judgment, 1534-1541.

148   FRESCOES ACCORDING TO REGION

Rome, Vatican, Cappella Paolina, Michelangelo, The Conversion of Saul and The Crucifixion of St. Peter, 1542-1549.
Rome, Santa Maria in Antiqua, frescoes in Byzantine style, dating back to 7-8C.
Rome, San Clemente, Lower Church, Life of St. Clement and Life of St. Alexius, end 11C. Upper Church, Cappella Baranda Castiglione, Masolino da Panicale and Masaccio, Life of St. Catherine of Alexandria and Life of St. Ambrose, 1425-1431.
Rome, SS. Quattro Coronati, Cappella San Silvestro, fresco cycle The Donation of Emperor Constantine, mid 13C.
Rome, Santa Cecilia in Trastevere, Pietro Cavallini, The Last Judgment, part of fresco cycle, 1295-1298.
Rome, San Giorgio al Velabro, apse painting attributed to Pietro Cavallini, end 13C.
Rome, Santa Maria sopra Minerva, Cappella Carafa, Filippino Lippi, Annunciation and Assumption of the Virgin Mary, The Dispute of Thomas Aquinas, and the Miracle of the Book, 1488-1490.
Rome, S. Maria in Vallicella, dome and apse, Pietro da Cortona, Holy Trinity and Assumption, 1647-1651.
Rome, Santa Maria in Aracoeli, Cappella Bufalini, Pinturicchio, Life of St. Bernardino of Siena, 1486.
Rome, Santa Maria del Popolo, Pinturicchio, frescoes in the first, third and fourth chapel on the right and on the vault behind the choir, 1484-1492.
Rome, Santa Maria della Pace, Cappella Chigi, Raphael, Four Sibyls receiving angelic instruction, 1514; Cappella Cesi, Rosso Fiorentino, Creation of Eve and Original Sin, 1524.

Rome, Sant'Agostino, Raphael, Prophet Isaiah, 1512.
Rome, Villa Farnesina, Sala di Galatea, Sebastiano del Piombo, Raphael, Baldassare Peruzzi; Loggia di Amore e Psiche, Raphael and assistants; Sala delle Prospettive, Peruzzi; Camera da letto, Il Sodoma, Life of Alexandre the Great, 1508-1520.
Rome, Villa Borghese, Giovanni Lanfranco, ceiling, The Gods of Olympus, 1624-1625.
Rome, Palazzo Barberini, Pietro da Cortona, The Allegory of Divine Providence and Barberini Power, 1633-1639.
Rome, Palazzo Farnese, ceiling, Annibale Carracci, The Loves of the Gods, 1597-1606.
Rome, San Luigi dei Francesi, Domenichino, Life of Saint Cecilia, 1612-1615.
Rome, Palazzo Pamphili, Gallery vault, Pietro da Cortona, Life of Aeneas, 1651.
Rome, Il Gesù, vault, Giovanni Battista Gaulli, Triumph of the Sacred Name of Jesus, 1674-1679.
Rome, Sant'Ignazio, vault, Andrea Pozzo, Apotheosis of St. Ignatius, 1691-1694.
Rome, Casino Ludovisi, Guercino, Aurora, 1621-1623.
Rome, Palazzo Pallavicini, Casino Rospiglioso, Guido Reni, Aurora, 1614
Rome, Sant' Andrea della Valle, dome, Giovanni Lanfranco, Glory of the Virgin Mary, 1625-1627.
Subiaco, Monastery (Sacro Speco) Upper Church. frescoes by the Sienese school in the 14th century, and frescoes from the early 15C relating to St. Benedict. The frescoes in the transept by the school of Umbria and the Marches. Lower Church, frescoes of the 13th century.

Southern Italy
Campania-Basilicata-Apulia-Calabria-Sicily

Alcamo, Santa Maria Assunta, vault and dome, 38 frescoes by Guglielmo Borremans, about 1715.

Brindisi, Santa Maria del Casale, above entrance: Rinaldo da Taranto, Last Judgment, early 14C.

Caltanissetta, Duomo, vault frescoes by Borremans, 1720; also frescoes by Borremans in the church of Santa Agata.

Capua, abbey of Sant' Angelo in Formis, nave and apse, scenes from the Old and New Testament, Last Judgment and Christ in Majesty, last quarter 11C.

Carpignano Salentino (Lecce), Cripta delle Ss. Marina e Cristina, frescoes 11-12C.

Casarano (Lecce), Santa Maria della Croce, Deesis, Scenes of the Passion and the lives of St. Catherine and St. Margaret, 11-13C.

Catania, Duomo, sacristy, Portrayal of the Mount Etna eruption in 1669.

Catania, San Benedetto, Giovanni Tuccari, frescoes in nave and chancel, about 1740.

Catania Palazzo Biscari, Feasts Hall, frescoes by Matteo Desiderato and Sabastiano Lo Monaco, Glories of the Paternó Castello di Biscari Family, 18C.

Galatina, Santa Caterina d'Alessandria, Life of St. Catherine, biblical scenes, Life of the Virgin Mary, Visions of the Apocalypse, 1415-1430.

Massafra, rupestrian churches of San Marco, the Cappella-cripta della Candelora and Cripta di San Leonardo, votive frescoes 12-14C.

Matera, rupestrian churches of Santa Barbara, Santa Maria d'Idris, Santa Lucia, frescoes 13C.
Melfi, cave church Santa Margherita, Meeting of the three living and the three dead, lives of saints, 13C.
Modica, San Nicolò Inferiore, Christ Pantocrator and saints, 13-14C.
Mottola, Cave church San Nicola a Casalrotto, Christ Pantocrator and votive frescoes,11-13C.
Naples, Duomo, Cappella del Tesoro di San Gennaro, Domenichino, Life of San Gennaro, 1631-1641.
Naples, San Paolo Maggiore, nave and sacristy, frescoes by Francesco Solimena, 1690.
Naples, Santa Maria Incoronata, Roberto Oderisi, The Triumph of Faith and Seven Sacraments, 1352.
Naples, San Gregorio Armeno, Luca Giordano, Life of St. Gregory, 1610.
Naples, Santa Maria Donnaregina, chancel, Pietro Cavallini, Stories of life of Christ, Apostles and saints, Last Judgment, 1307-1320.
Naples, Monastero San Martino, frescoes by Caracciolo, Micco Spadaro, Luca Giordano, 17C.
Nicosia, San Vincenzo Ferreri, apse, Borremans, The Glory of San Vincenzo Ferreri, 1717.
Otranto, San Pietro, Saints and biblical scenes, 13-15C.
Padula, Certosa di San Lorenzo, refectory, Alessio d'Elia, The wedding feast at Cana, 1749.
Palermo, San Giuseppe dei Teatini, vault and dome frescoes by Borremans, 18C.
Palermo, Palazzo Abatellis (Galleria Regionale di Sicilia), Triumph of Death, mid 15C.

Palermo, Chiesa dei 40 Martiri alla Guilla, vault frescoes by Borremans, 1720; also frescoes by Borremans in the Chiesa Santa Maria delle Grazie di Montevergini.

Ripacandida, Santuario di San Donato, biblical scenes, lives of saints, 14C.

Rivello, Monastery Sant'Antonio, Girolamo Todisco, Crucifixion of the franciscan martyrs in Japan, 16C; also frescoes by Todisco in the cloister; in the refectory, Last Supper by Pietrafesa, 1559.

Tursi, Santa Maria Maggiore, Girolamo Todisco, legends of saints, 1550.

Tursi, Santa Maria di Anglona, nave, scenes from the Old and New Testament, 14C.

Venosa, Abbazia della SS. Trinità, votive frescoes, Pietà with donor John I of Naples, 14C.

Maps

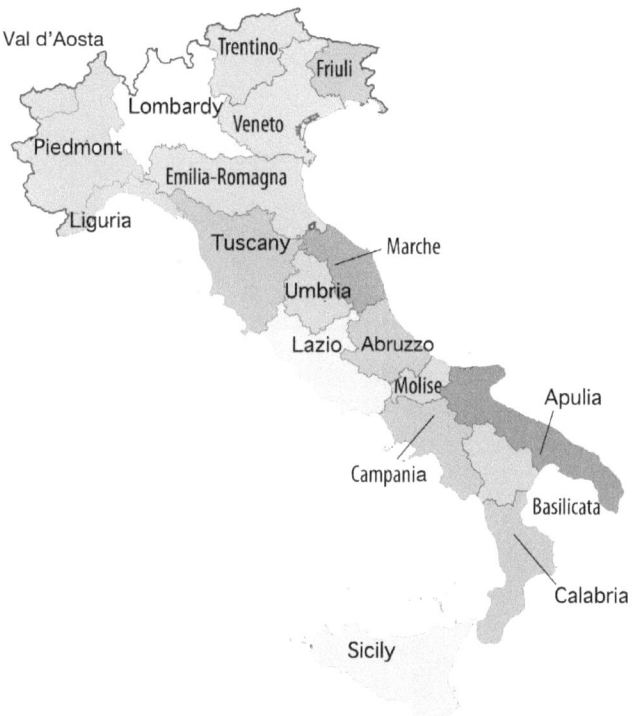

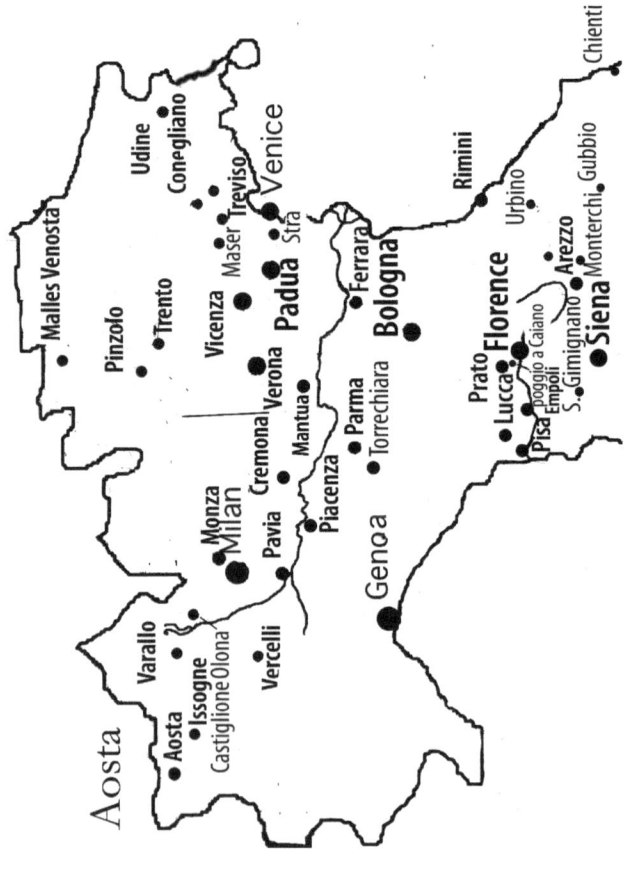

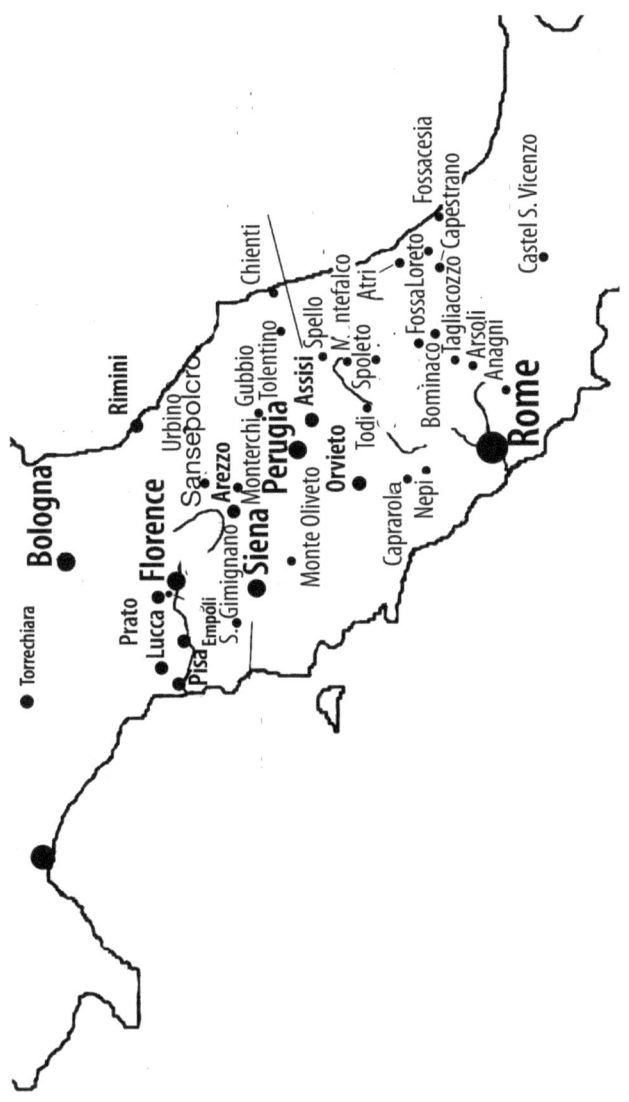

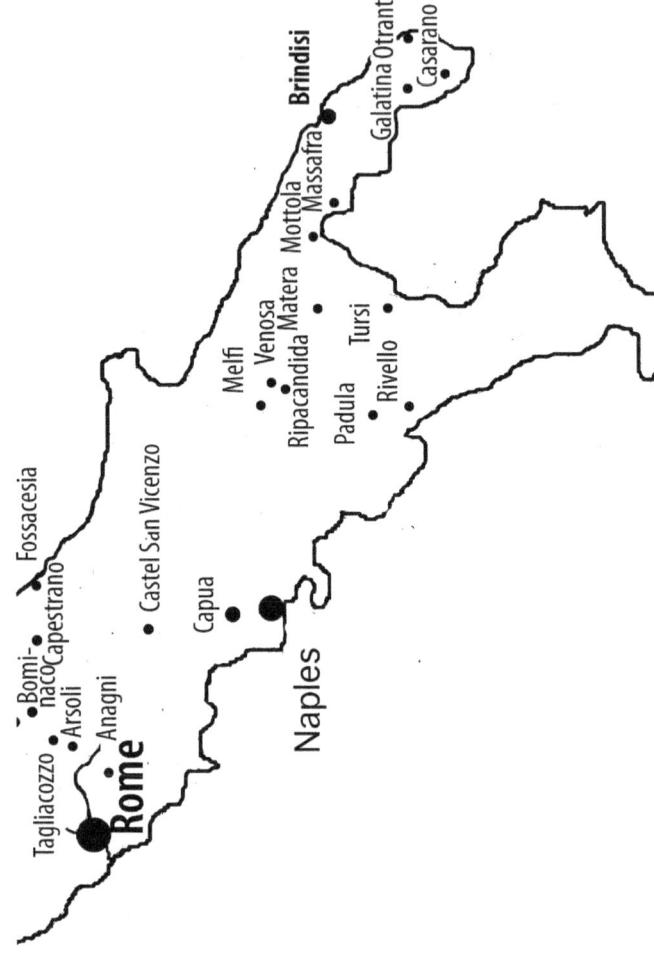

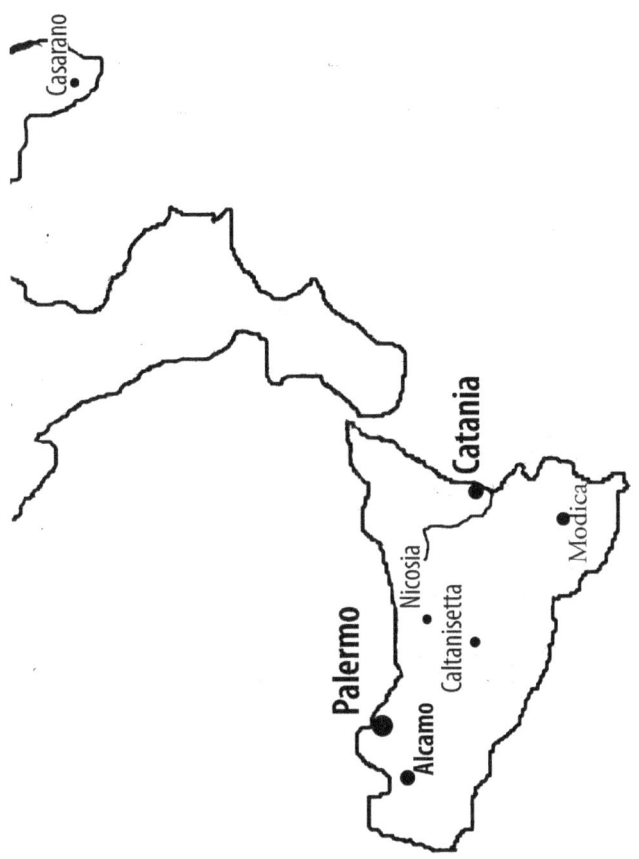